ALICE E. SINK

Wicked Lexington, North Carolina

THE History PRESS

Published by The History Press
Charleston, SC 29403
www.historypress.net

First published 2011
Second printing 2015

Manufactured in the United States

ISBN 978.1.60949.309.7

Library of Congress Cataloging-in-Publication Data

Sink, Alice E.
Wicked Lexington, North Carolina / Alice Sink.
p. cm.
Includes bibliographical references.
ISBN 978-1-60949-309-7
1. Crime--North Carolina--Lexington--History--Anecdotes. 2. Corruption--North Carolina--Lexington--History--Anecdotes. 3. Criminals--North Carolina--Lexington--Biography--Anecdotes. 4. Lexington (N.C.)--History--Anecdotes. 5. Lexington (N.C.)--Social conditions--Anecdotes. 6. Lexington (N.C.)--Moral conditions--Anecdotes. 7. Lexington (N.C.)--Biography--Anecdotes. I. Title.
HV6795.L49S46 2011
364.109756'68--dc22
2011013957

Praise for Alice Sink's Writing

"Sink has taken her memories and channeled them into five years of research and writing that resulted in her book *The Grit Behind the Miracle*, which chronicles the true story of the Infantile Paralysis Hospital that was built in 54 hours in 1944." Jill Doss-Raines, the *Dispatch*

"Throughout the rare glimpses from 1900 to around the early 1950s, Sink stuck to one consistent theme in *Kernersville*. Sink portrayed the sense of community." Brandon Keel, *Kernersville News*

"Community abounds in a colorful new book about the history of North Carolina boardinghouses—a traveler's guide to a lost place that was small-town and worldly at the same time." Lorraine Ahearn, *Greensboro News & Record*

"A very highly recommended addition for academic and community library collections, *Boarding House Reach* could serve as a template for similar studies for other state." *Midwest Book Review*

"*Boarding House Reach* reminds us of one of the most important truths of life: There are no ordinary people! Every story here is fascinating—and every one importantly belongs to history." Fred Chappell

"*Hidden History of the Piedmont Triad* recounts a number of interesting stories from throughout the Triad—from historic people and places to lesser-known colorful slices of life." Jimmy Tomlin, *High Point Enterprise*

"In *Hidden History of the Piedmont Triad*, Sink writes about Lexington's downtown dime stores. She describes how each counter was like a different department of the store, with a candy counter and comic book section popular with children…and makeup counters that carried old-fashioned items such as Tangee lipstick and Evening in Paris perfume." Vikki Broughton Hodges, the *Dispatch*

"Did you know that a nightclub in High Point once hosted the likes of Ella Fitzgerald and Duke Ellington? Have you heard the story of Lexington native, John Andrew Roman, put to death on circumstantial evidence, or the local World War II fighter plane pilot who flew eighty-two missions to prevent German fighters from attacking American bombers? Therse are but three of the many little-known stories…found in *Hidden History of the Piedmont Triad*." *Arbor Lamplighter*

"[*Hidden History of the Piedmont Triad*]...covers people, places and events that have been forgotten." Ryan Gay, lifestyles editor, *Kernersville News*

"In *Hidden History of the Piedmont Triad*, author Alice Sink rediscovers the quirky stories of the Piedmont Triad...tying North Carolina into the rest of world history." *Our State Magazine*

"*Hidden History of Hilton Head* offers a lively array of historical tidbits and tales. From beautiful poems written by renowned locals to the songs that guided the slaves to freedom and time-tested regional recipes, author Alice Sink's collection truly encompasses the spirit of the Lowcountry" The History Press (Charleston, SC)

"The premise of *No [Wo]man Is an Island* is outstanding! I laughed out loud—even hollered a few times...don't remember doing that since *Raney* and *Walking Across Egypt.* I can see it as a TV sitcom if the PC police wouldn't kill it." Carol Branard

"Thank you for *Hidden History of the Western North Carolina Mountains*—which is not really hidden. I knew almost all the stories and information and even some of the recipes. But then I'm supposed to, as an old Haywood County boy. Great to see it all in a book!" Fred Chappell

For the Lexington Senior High School graduating class of 1958.
It was a very good group!

Contents

Foreword

Alice Evans Sink—remember the last name—has produced a very well-done work of writing and fact gathering that is much more than just the "wicked" in the title.

It's about Lexington and Davidson County, people and events, and as one born and raised in Davidson County, plus someone who spent forty-four years in and around the newsroom of the county's daily newspaper, I was surprised and pleased at all the new things I learned and the old things with which I was refamiliarized.

The interest it will raise in you is a tribute to Alice's work in producing it, and I hope you enjoy it. And there's some fun stuff in there too.

And about Alice's last name: as a disclaimer, I should tell you that we're related. She married my fifth cousin once removed, giving my family an upward thrust.

Joe Sink

PREFACE

A Word from the Author

I was born, reared, married and gave birth to my children in Lexington, North Carolina; in fact, I lived there all my life, except for the past twelve years. As a child, I sat on the front porch of my paternal Grandmother Evans's boardinghouse and listened to all the "town talk" from my aunts and the boarders. They never missed a beat! While pretending to play with my dolly, I was really taking in every word they were saying, storing the gossip in my brain, I suppose, until adulthood when I would become a published writer. Actually, although I did not remember actual names and dates when I started writing *Wicked Lexington, North Carolina*, the archives of the hometown newspaper, the *Dispatch*, gave me all the details I needed—and more!

I can still hear the loud, wicked volume of the town's electric siren, which announced "dinner hour" for factory and mill workers and also blew a certain number of times to give the townspeople a signal for the neighborhood where a fire truck would be heading through. This sometimes caused traffic problems because locals hopped in their cars or trucks and arrived at the scene about the same time as the firefighters.

Some of the articles in this book mention my uncle, Dr. G.C. Gambrell, county health officer, and his trips to the local jail to treat those incarcerated.

I was a Lexington neighbor of Frances Holt McKay, who invited me into her William R. Holt's Homestead home one day and showed me the upstairs bedroom door with iron brackets where the Holt daughters were kept safe from the Federal soldiers who occupied the house in 1865.

I remember when the Confederate Soldier Monument stood in the middle of the intersection of Main and Center Streets; cars moseyed around it, occasionally causing minor fender benders.

I was told to never venture by Do Drop Inn. I remember asking about the "white" and "colored" entrance doors to Stamey's Barbeque and separate water fountains in Belk's Department Store.

I have just recently been told that the house where Dudley Moore killed Mrs. Jacob Berrier is the same home purchased by my aunt, Mary Noble, and uncle, Harold, years later. I probably slept in the same bedroom where Mrs. Berrier was shot, but I never heard of that tragedy until years later.

When we were newlyweds, Tom and I lived at the corner of Fifth Avenue and State Street in Lexington, across the street from Sheriff Wilfred and Mrs. Eurnice Fritts, both mentioned in this book,

Although I did not attend the Elvis Presley concert at the YMCA, a short two blocks from my childhood home, many of my classmates went and talked about it for months afterward.

I vividly recall the terrible news of Mrs. Hinshaw's rape and murder. Her house was not far from ours—near Holt Moffit Field. My aunt, Mabel, who attended most events at Lexington's Davidson County Courthouse, took me with her to John Andrew Roman's trial. I could still pick out our two seats in the courtroom, but I was too young to remember many details. I do remember my aunt telling me, "You might learn something!"

Thinking back, I believe Aunt's Mabel's original children's story was probably another "first" for me in the "wicked" category. I still have this favorite story in Aunt Mabel's handwriting:

> *Once upon a time a little gray mouse and a little brown sausage loved each other so dearly that they decided to live together. They planned their work so that it could be done with the greatest of ease. They planned to take turn—and turn about—cooking the meals.*
>
> *Sausage took the first turn gladly. When the pan was ready, he jumped in happily, came to a nice brown on both sides, then jumped out again. Mousey could hardly wait to taste the food that smelled so good! Smacking his lips, he exclaimed, "How did you make it so tasty?"*
>
> *"With myself," answered the sausage. "When the pan was ready, I jumped in, relaxed long enough, then jumped out again. Mousey ate and ate and ate, smacking his lips happily.*
>
> *Next day when Mousey's turn came, he said to himself, "Now I must do as good a turn for my friend as he did for me. I think we'll have beans for dinner."*
>
> *When the sausage came home and didn't see Mousey, he called and called and called, "Mousey, Mousey, where are you?" No answer. Then he said to himself, "I'll just look in the pot and see what we're having for dinner."*
>
> *When he saw inside the pot, he cried and cried and cried, moaning, "Poor, poor Mousey! Too long in the cookery. My dear friend!"*

And to this day, if you listen very carefully when your mother fries sausage, you can hear, "Poor, poor Mousey, Poor, poor Mousey!"

Acknowledgements

When I had questions about specifics concerning *Wicked Lexington, North Carolina*, I asked Joe Sink, retired publisher of the *Dispatch*, what he remembered or had read. In fact, one of my favorite pieces in this book is Joe's talk, as presented to the O. Henry Study Club of Lexington. I appreciate his allowing me to print it here in its entirety.

To Chad Killebrew, executive editor of the *Dispatch*: many thanks for teaching me how to access all back issues of the newspaper in the archives.

For the knowledgeable folks at the Davidson County Museum, I deeply appreciate your interest and your assistance.

As always, to the librarians at High Point University's Smith Library: thanks for answering my many questions, securing requested interlibrary loans and teaching me how to install and use Jing, which allowed me to access, copy and print newspaper archives all the way back to the early 1900s. David, Mike, Bob and Nina: I could not have written this book without your help and your patience.

For husband Tom, who has shown great interest in this book about our hometown, for his careful proofreading of drafts, for suggestions and telephone calls he has made on the book's behalf and—as always—for "driving Miss Daisy" on research trips.

To my editor at The History Press, Jessica Berzon: let me thank you over and over for your belief in this publication, your great editorial advice and your on-the-spot assistance with my many questions. I especially honor your request that I not go beyond 1969 in my research and subsequent writing of this book. Thanks to Amber Allen, project editor, who kept reminding me to use Chicago Manual of Style, fifteenth edition. To Katie Parry and Dan Watson, my publicists at The History Press, and to Jamie Barreto, a VIP in sales: you are the ones who "make it happen."

CHAPTER 1

Now You Know

Elvis Presley: Our Mothers Were Shocked!

Elvis rolled into Lexington just before dawn on Wednesday, March 21, 1956, "carrying a tenacious flu and a bout of nausea with him." He was also bringing with him something never before seen in Lexington: suggestive hip movements and sexy gyrations.

> *His gyrations are usually described as "actin' like his jeans was on fire, shaggin, wifflin', jazzin' it up, etc. These are all evasive ways of saying that Elvis accompanies his singing with the motions usually associated with the sex act. In burlesque parlance, they're known as bumps and grinds—but a strip-teaser who tried to emulate Elvis would probably end up in the hoosegow. Because he writhes with such an unnatural frenzy he is frequently accused of taking dope or being drunk. Neither is true. As his manager says, "That boy don't need a stimulant, he needs soothin' syrup."*

According to various historians and newspaper articles, this series of events introduced Elvis to Lexington:

> *After checking into the New Lexington Hotel on North Main Street and sleeping for several hours, Elvis went to Leonard's Cleaners for laundry and Elvis also got a lesson in typing Windsor knots from the owner, Don*

Leonard. Back at the Hotel, Elvis was examined by Dr. Milton E. Block, diagnosed with a mild case of the flu and given two prescriptions.

The show, in the meantime, had sold out and they had turned away more than 2000 people. Dr. L.C. Harpe, Don Leonard and Haynes Sherron were waiting at the YMCA for Elvis. They were to serve as his bodyguards downstairs and in his dressing room. About 6:30 Elvis arrived and the men met him in the parking lot. The girls began closing in on him as he emerged from the car. The men were able to get him inside and down to his dressing room. Elvis then gave Dr. Harpe a note from Omar Davis. The note instructed Elvis to see and talk to Dr. Harpe for a few minutes. Dr. Harpe asked Elvis to autograph a program for him. A photographer snapped a picture of Elvis posing with his body guards. While in the dressing room, Elvis asked Don Leonard to help him with his necktie one more time. Mr. Leonard helped Elvis tie the Windsor knot and adjust it one last time. Elvis was not even supposed to be at the Lexington "Y" on March 21, 1956. Eddy Arnold had been booked initially by Oscar Davis with Lexington's Civitan Club; however, about a week before that scheduled concert "Colonel Parker contacted the YMCA's general secretary, Carl Link, and told him that Eddy Arnold would not be able to appear… but that he was sending a young singer named Elvis Presley instead." That notification of change caused some concern with those involved:

Dr. Harpe, Civitan president, expressed concern about whether they would make any money on an unheard singer's performance. Colonel Parker told Dr. Harpe, "I'll tell you what. I'll give you fifty percent of the gate or I'll give you a guaranteed flat fee of two hundred dollars." Not having heard of Elvis, Dr. Harpe told Colonel Parker, "We'd better take the two hundred dollars. At least that's a sure thing."

On March 15, 1956, the *Dispatch* ran the following article and Elvis's picture, playing his guitar with legs spread:

"New Singing Sensation Elvis Presley, Others To Appear Here at 'Y'"

Elvis Presley, great new singing sensation who has skyrocketed to the top practically overnight, will appear in person headlining a big show Wednesday, March 21, at the YMCA-Gymnasium for one big show at 8:00. Appearing with him are Mother Maybelle and the Carter Sisters, featuring June Carter, Rod Brasfield, Hal and Ginger and others. Presley, just turned twenty-one, is called the greatest new personality in the last ten years of recorded music. About two years ago, Elvis stopped in a recording studio in his home town of

Memphis, Tennessee, to make a demonstration record of his voice, which he could play for his folks and friends. Six months later, the recording manager called him up to ask him if he wanted to make some records for sale to the public—and that is when things started to happen.

From his very first release, it was apparent that Elvis had what the record buyers wanted, and each successive record release outsold the previous one. RCA Victor Records, when advised of the excitement he was causing among the teen-age audiences, paid $40,0000.00 for his recording contract.

He is one of the few artists to have records played by Country, Pop, and Blues disc jockies [sic]. *On his personal appearances, he is breaking records whenever he shows. The reaction to his appearances on the stage show portion of the Jackie Gleason TV show were phenomenal. Presley is said to have become the idol of the teen-agers today, just as Frank Sinatra captured the bobby soxers some years ago. Hollywood movie makers have not missed out, for he is soon to make a screen test for one of the major studios.*

Elvis makes his home with his folks in Memphis, Tennessee. He is very proud of his Mom and Dad, and when on the road, does not fail to make that daily call home.

The day before Elvis's performance, the *Dispatch* ran another enticing article:

Advance tickets are moving at a fast clip and a big attendance should be on hand to "rock and roll" with Elvis Presley, youthful singing sensation the YMCA tomorrow night.

Presley, the atomic-driven "Mr. Dynamite" of the entertainment world, heads an all-star show that starts at 8 o'clock. Just turned twenty-one, Presley is called the greatest new personality in the last ten years of recorded music. He has best sellers in a number of divisions of RCA recordings, has made many radio and television appearances and is soon booked for a trip to Hollywood to make movies.

His best selling record right now is "Heartbreak Hotel." Other favorites are "I Was the One," "I Forgot to Remember to Forget, "Good Rocking' Tonight, "Tutti Fruitti" and "Blue Suede Shoes."

A gay dresser and full of energy, Presley is a great one of public appearances. His restless motions while singing have gained him acclaim from many sources. He is a favorite of the teen-aged set and scores of youngsters are expected to watch him work tomorrow night.

Presley appears here at the head of an outstanding show that also includes such favorites as Mother Mabelle and the Carter sisters and the comedy ace of Grand Ole Opry, Rod Brasfield. All of these stars have been seen on television many times.

Advance tickets are being sold at the James Harman Music Company on North Main Street and are moving at a good clip according to Mr. Hartman. The price range is a popular one. $1 for general admission and $1.50 for reserved seats.

The *Dispatch* ran the following article the day after Elvis's performance:

A whirlwind blew into Lexington last night, attracted a record turnout of spectators at the spacious YMCA arena, and left this morning on the way to Richmond, Va. and another show. The whirlwind is Elvis Presley, 21-year-old singing sensation of the nation who has what many experts describe as the "biggest drawing power in the entertainment world at present." Elvis came to Lexington yesterday morning, slept most of the day in a hotel, woke up to find he was running a fever, called a local physician for treatment and went on as scheduled at the YMCA last night.

"I have a mild case of the flu," the "Mr. Dynamite" of recording fame said last night in his dressing room. "I guess I should rest some but my friends are coming out to see me and the show must go on." And the show did go on. Elvis in natty attire, went to the stage to feature the second part of an all-star review. He had to be ushered from the dressing room by policemen who forced their way through scores of young girls seeking autographs, souvenirs or just a look at "their boy."

On March 21, 2006, fifty years to the day after Elvis's only appearance in Lexington, the *Dispatch* published an article that contained the remembrances of some of the local residents that had attended the concert:

"Our mothers were interested in seeing Maybelle Carter," recalled Glenda Hartley, then a junior at Reeds High School, who went with her good friend, Janet Bame. "Of course, my friend and I were interested in seeing Elvis." Hartley laughed as she recalled Elvis' notorious hips and the reaction of the parents in attendance. "I had never seen anything comparable," Hartley said. "Our mothers were shocked."

"My friends were yelling and screaming, but I wasn't, because I wanted to hear," said Sue Kearns Haltom, who the next day would become the envy of her squealing pack of companions when she informed them that she had gotten Presley's autograph in the lobby of the New Lexington Hotel, where

Elvis Presley. *Courtesy of Wikimedia.*

the performer and his entourage had stayed. "When the other girls found out, they could've killed us," she said.

Nancy Robbins and her friends were cruising the streets of Lexington after the show when they saw an incredible, unlikely sight: Elvis Presley, sitting at the counter of the March Hotel's coffee shop, all by himself. Her friends were too timid to talk to him, but Robbins, the brave one, stepped through the front door and introduced herself. After she "sort of cornered him," in her words, the two talked for about five uninterrupted minutes. "He wanted to know what grade I was in," she said. "He said he missed school, and he didn't know how he was going to like all this touring." And what was it like talking to a man who shaped the course of modern music? "He was shy. He was almost to the point of being bashful," Robbins said. She said farewell after getting his autograph on a small calendar she was carrying, got a kiss on the cheek and walked back into the cool March evening with an Elvis story for the ages.

Elvis Presley's March 21, 1956 appearance at the Lexington YMCA was complete with his intricate motions, his caressing and making love to his guitar as he swirled his hips, along with adults' accusations of his "selling sex with cold, deliberate calculation." An elderly lady asked Elvis if he wasn't ashamed of his act's vulgarity. His response was, "M'am I ain't being vulgar. I'm jus' jumpin' with the beat, 'cause the jumpin's in me. How in the peapickin' world kin I help it if I go wi-aud when I sing? That's the way I feel."

And the mothers in the audience were shocked!

IT MUST HAVE BEEN THE COFFEE

Nannie Doss has been called the "Jolly Black Widow" serial killer. Lexington was definitely not her first stop or her last, but she met her soon-to-be third husband while visiting there:

> *He was Arlie Lanning and she married him within three days of meeting him through another lonely hearts column. Lanning was in many ways like his predecessor, Harrelson: he was an alcoholic and a womanizer. However, in the marriage, it was Doss who often disappeared for months on end. When she was at home, however, she played a doting housewife, and when her husband died of what was said to be heart failure, the whole town turned up to his funeral in support of her. Afterwards, the house the couple lived in burned to the ground. It had been left to Lanning's sister, and had it survived it would have gone to her. As it happened, the insurance money went to Doss, and she quickly banked it. She soon left North Carolina, but only after Lanning's elderly mother had died in her sleep. She ended up at her sister Dovie's home. Dovie was bedridden and soon after Doss's arrival she died.*
>
> *Known as The Giggling Nanny, The Giggling Granny, Arsenic Annie and The Jolly Black Widow, Doss was born in Alabama in 1906 and grew up with a strict, controlling and nasty father. She suffered headaches and depression, which the family thought came from a train accident when she was seven years old. As a teen, she entertained herself with romance magazines and lonely hearts columns. Her father did not allow her to wear attractive outfits or makeup; she could not attend social events.*
>
> *When she was only sixteen years old, she married Charlie Braggs, and they had four daughters. When two of the girls died from suspected food poison, Braggs reportedly fled, taking the oldest daughter Melvina with him and leaving the baby behind. Nannie and Charlie divorced in 1928, and Melvina returned to lived with her mother.*
>
> *Nannie's second marriage was to Robert (Frank) Harrelson, and despite his alcoholism, the marriage lasted sixteen years until drunk Harrelson raped Doss. She poisoned his corn whiskey with rat poison. Subsequently, Harrelson's death that same evening was agonizing.*
>
> *Melvina married and gave birth to a son, Robert Lee Haynes, in 1943. When Robert was two years old, he was under Nannie's care when he died mysteriously. The cause of his death was "asphyxia from unknown causes." Nanny then collected the $500 life insurance she had taken out on the child. When Melvina gave birth to a baby girl, who died soon after*

birth, Melvina told her husband and her sister Florine that she had seen her mother stick a hatpin into the baby's head. Medical personnel could not explain the baby's death.

Nannie's fourth husband was Richard L. Morton, a womanizer. She poisoned his mother first and three months later, Morton died from poison.

Samuel Doss, Nannie's fifth husband, became ill with a severe digestive tract infection. After he was released from the hospital, "Nannie killed him that evening in her rush to collect the two life insurance policies they had taken out on him." Nannie was arrested after Samuel's autopsy revealed a huge amount of arsenic in his system." What happened next?

Nannie confessed to killing four of her husbands, her mother, her sister Dovie, her grandson Robert and her mother-in-law, Arlie Lanning's mother in Lexington. The state of Oklahoma centered its case only on Samuel Doss. The prosecution found her mentally fit for trial. Nannie pleaded guilty on May 17, 1955, and was sentenced to life imprisonment. The state did not pursue the death penalty due to her gender. Doss was never charged with the other deaths. She died of leukemia in the hospital ward of Oklahoma State Penitentiary in 1965.

Now that we have become acquainted with Nannie Doss's personality and character, along with the poisoning of four husbands, mother, sister, grandson and mother-in-law, let's focus more on her life in Lexington with her third husband, Arlie Lanning, as reported by Sherby Green, Nannie's descendant and armchair biographer:

Wherever Nannie roamed after Harrelson's death, she eventually wound up in the scenic little town of Lexington, North Carolina, in response to another lonely-hearts column. The year was 1947 and the husband-to-be this time was laborer Arlie Lanning, an ex-Alabaman. After meeting her for the first time, the couple married two days later. Tongue-in-cheek, writer Terry Manners asserts, "Arlie believed their marriage was set in heaven, where he was later to be dispatched."

Life with Arlie wasn't as dramatically chaotic as it had been with Harrelson, partly because for most of the time Nannie wasn't home. Whereas, her former spouse had been the prodigal, Nannie now mimicked him. Whenever things got hectic, whenever Arlie drank too much and flirted too much—he, too, like his predecessor, loved his alcohol and his females—Nannie pulled the suitcase from her closet and went away to parts unknown, sometimes for months on end. She would leave without a word.

Ladies' tea. *Courtesy of the Library of Congress.*

Or maybe she would leave a message on a crumpled piece of paper under the salt shaker. "Gone." Occasionally, Arlie would receive a cablegram, "Send money" or "Be home soon." The wires came from all directions; she seemed not to remain in one place too long; she simply darted as if on an escape route from responsibility.

Out of the blue she would come home. Arlie, not brutal like Frank had been, would merely shrug a hello; that is, if he wasn't unconscious on the sofa from drink. For a while, he and Nannie would play loving couple. He knew the reason she took flight so often was because—or so she claimed—his drinking binges and his womanizing. So, upon her return, he always committed to the dry wagon, a promise that she, and probably he too, knew would be busted maybe days, weeks or, if luck was with them, months ahead.

When on the home front, Nannie acted the perfect wife for the benefit of her neighbors. Her trips away would be explained as visits to friends and family; in part they were true, for Nannie would occasionally bus to Gadsden, Alabama, to tend to her sister Dovie who had contracted cancer, or visit Arlie's 84-year-old mother who lived in a nearby town and needed help housecleaning and canning.

Evidence of a domestic woman were there for all the Lexington neighbors to see: aroma of apple pie cooling on the window sill, fresh laundry lemon-

> *scented hanging on the backyard line, a manicured garden, and lace curtains in all the front windows. At night she would read her monthly* True Romance *or a novel she had picked up at a community rummage sale. She wasn't literate and her vocabulary was minimal, so the books she chose to read were basic and a little tawdry; of well-built heroes and shapely dames caught in at least one love triangle that usually contained several scenes in a boudoir.*

It later became obvious to friend and neighbors that Nannie always presented a charming front to the folks of Lexington:

> *In Lexington, Nannie was an avid churchgoer and she had become intimate with the minister's family and many of the families in the Methodist congregation. Arlie Lanning, during sober periods, would accompany his wife to Sunday morning services and remain at her side afterwards for the tea socials and picnics hosted by the ladies auxiliary, to which Nannie belonged. But, there were whispers among the attendees at these functions, generated by the presence of Mr. Lanning. His reputation, to be blunt, preceded him. Before and during his marriage to Nannie he was often seen in the lower Lexington dives with one of the floozies who hung there. Arlie was a rapscallion, said the fine people of the Lexington Methodist Church, and poor Nannie…well, they didn't know if she was aware of his maneuverings, but be it far from them to break her heart. Behind closed doors in quiet conversation, Lanning was the town's villain, she its travelling martyr.*

When the town of Lexington turned out for Arlie's funeral in February 1950, "it was out of great respect for the heart broken widow, not the corpse," as explained by one historian:

> *Yes, Arlie had died suddenly. Cause: heart failure. Of course, there was something that had caused the heart to fail, the doctor said, but in cases like Arlie's, where there was absolutely no reason for suspicion, it would be superfluous to conduct an autopsy. Any number of things could have caused him to lie in pain as he did for a couple of days before succumbing. Most likely, it had been the dangerous flu virus that had been sweeping the state, striking some people worse than others. He had had all the symptoms—sweating, vomiting, dizziness—and after all, the doctor admitted, Arlie's body was not in the best shape, his stomach already half gone with the drink, his heart already weakened.*

Nannie played right into the doctors' diagnosis as she talked with Lexington neighbors:

"He just sat down one morning to drink a cup of coffee and eat a bowl of prunes I especially prepared for him," Nannie admitted to her neighbors gathered around his coffin. "Up until then, why let me tell you, he looked in fine shape. Then...well...two days later...dead. I nursed him, believe me, I nursed him, but I failed."

And for an extra touch, she dabbed her eyes with her kerchief.

"Poor, poor Arlie. You know what he said to me before he breathed his last? 'Nannie,' he said, 'Nannie, it must have been the coffee.'"

ANNIE OAKLEY: TRAIN WRECK THAT CHANGED HER LIFE

The date was October 29, 1901, and the notable train wreck happened about 3:00 a.m. at Linwood, near Lexington. Members of Buffalo Bill's Wild West Show were in two trains headed to Danville, Virginia, for its last performance of the season when the accident occurred. This is what happened:

Annie Oakley: famous for her rifle shot. *Courtesy of the Library of Congress.*

When the first section passed the switching station, the switcher thought that it was the whole outfit, so he threw the switch. The second section ran into an oncoming train. The wooden cars became so many piles of kindling as people and animals cried out in pain and steam hissed. Legend says that Annie Oakley, now 41, was found pinned beneath the rubble and it took several hours before she could be extracted. As Li'l Missie was carried by stretcher past some wounded horses that had to be shot, she supposedly remarked that she felt sorry for them. Just 17 hours after the wreck, according to legend, her brown hair turned totally white because of the horror of the accident.

Whirling Hawk, a Sioux Indian from Buffalo Bill's Wild West Show. *Courtesy of the Library of Congress.*

Shirl Kasper, biographer of Annie Oakley, and an article in the *Charlotte Observer* both contend that Annie did not suffer serious injuries. Kasper also has a different opinion about Annie's hair:

> *While Annie's hair did turn white rather fast, it wasn't because of the train wreck. Two newspaper articles in Annie's scrapbooks at the Buffalo Bill*

Left: Charging Thunder, a Sioux Indian from Buffalo Bill's Wild West Show. *Courtesy of the Library of Congress.*

Right: William F. Cody, aka "Buffalo Bill." *Courtesy of the Library of Congress.*

> *Historical Center say that her hair turned white after she sat too long in a hot bath at a health resort later that year. In any case…it was her white hair, not any bodily injuries, that convinced Annie Oakley to immediately leave Buffalo Bill's Wild West.*

This One Made It to the *New York Times*!

Robert Baxter McRary was born on November 21, 1860, in Lexington, North Carolina. His background is interesting and varied:

> *Among other things, Robert Baxter McRary was a school teacher, a principal, an administrator in the NC public school system, a public servant and a business man. For 6 years he served as the city magistrate in Lexington, NC. Robert Baxter McRary also served as a trustee of Lincoln University from 1931–1946. He is renowned for his grace of manner and dress, his elegance, and the effectiveness of his public and*

> *private speaking in the Methodist Episcopal Church. From his early days in the preparatory department in 1880 to his death in 1946, while serving as trustee he maintained a great love for LU, expressed loyal service and gave generous gifts to the university. Through his last will and testament he provided for the erection of "the Robert Baxter McRary memorial building."*

The *New York Times*'s August 17, 1920 edition published the following article entitled, "Accuses Wife and Negro: North Carolina Editor Asks Divorce and $100,000 Damages":

> *Henry B. Varner, former President of the National Editorial Association, ex-Commissioner of Labor and Printing, now Chairman of the State Prison Board, has brought suit for $100,000 against R. Baxter McRary of Lexington, Grand Master of the North Carolina negro Masons, and perhaps the best-known negro in the State, for alleged alienation of Mrs. Varner's affections. He has also sued his wife for absolute divorce.*
>
> *Monday night, when Varner was in New York, citizens saw McRary enter the Varner home. They surrounded it. When they threw flashlight on the cellar he tried to escape, but was caught under the floor. He was arrested and warned by Mayor Hedrick to flee. Immediately Varner attached all the McRary property and entered the suit. Mrs. Varner returned to her old home in Kentucky. The court proceedings have been started in Lexington, where the Varners and McRary live. The complaint alleges that McRary set out to destroy Varner's domestic happiness and accomplished it. McRary has been prominent in social reforms for his race. As public speaker he has few equals in the State.*
>
> *McRary was born a slave, but by thrift became the owner of the property on which his white masters lived, and amassed about the largest fortune of any North Carolina negro. Varner was elected President of the National Editorial Association after twice being chosen President of the State association. He had been a candidate for Congress in the Seventh District and has held the Chairmanship of the Prison Board eight years. He is owner and editor of the Lexington Dispatch. Mrs. Varner was prominent socially as a club-woman and church worker. She and Mr. Varner were married twenty years ago.*

CARNIVAL MEN VERSUS DINER THIEF

The article with a caption boldly declaring "Carnival Men Assist in Arrest of Diner Thief Here This Morn" made the front page of the *Dispatch*'s July 22, 1949 edition. A subcaption—"Showmen Pick Up Local Man After He Raided Diner, Summon Police"—introduces this story:

> *Members of the Davidson County sheriff's department this morning credited two carnival men with great assistance in the apprehension of a man now being held in jail here on larceny charges.*
>
> *Deputy Sheriff H.C. Koonts states Charlie Richardson, local man, aged about thirty five, was arrested about five o'clock this morning after he was stopped on the Southern railway tracks near Highway 29, south of the city by M.T. Akers and Bill Forcum of Stan Brothers Shows, now operating on Highway 29 under Amvet sponsorship.*
>
> *Deputy Koonts states Richardson admitted entering Freedle's diner near the carnival location and taking a quantity of merchandise. Richardson is being held in jail and bond is set at $3,000 for his release.*
>
> *The deputy sheriff said he received a call about 5:10 reporting the breaking and entering and he immediately went to the carnival lot where he found Akers and Forcum alone with Richardson.*
>
> *Koonts said Akers told him he saw Richardson around the carnival hut early this morning and later saw him enter the diner. He said a short time later he saw the man walking up the railroad tracks with some goods, and after calling Forcum, who was sleeping in a trailer, Richardson was stopped.*
>
> *It was reported Richardson had been drinking and admitted taking goods from the diner.*
>
> *Deputy Koonts said entry had been made in the building through a window and eleven handkerchiefs, twenty-one bars of candy, fifteen packages of cigarettes, a box of cigars, one flashlight, some pennies and a bread knife were recovered.*
>
> *The officer stated Richardson's hand was cut when he was picked up and some blood was found on the inside of the diner.*
>
> *Last night Richardson was reported to have helped out some at the diner by sweeping the floors for a package of cigarettes.*
>
> *After his arrest Richardson was placed in jail on charges of breaking and entering and larceny and receiving. He will receive hearing in County court here next week.*

Davidson Jury Does Not Believe Girl's Story of Attack

According to a February 4, 1925 newspaper article, a jury acquitted Everett Gordon on a charge of criminal assault brought by sixteen-year-old Miss Edith Albright, sister of Gordon's wife. Apparently, many details were exposed during the trial:

> *Miss Edith Albright, accuser of Gordon, testified that she was sixteen last June and a sister of Gordon's wife. On November 26 last she said she was at home alone about eleven o'clock in the morning when Gordon, who lives only about 100 yards away, came to her home and asked to get some smoking tobacco from the small store the Albright house, kept by the witness' brother. Her father was employed in High Point, her mother had gone to that city and her brother was away from home temporarily, a state of facts she said Gordon ascertained by questioning her.*
>
> *Miss Albright said she got the key and unlocked the store, secured the smoking tobacco and charged it to Gordon, who went toward home. In about five minutes he returned and said he wanted chewing tobacco also. Expressing doubt there was any in the store, she said she again unlocked the building but found no tobacco.*

According to Miss Albright's testimony, this is where the trouble started:

> *Gordon came behind the counter where she was and looked under the counter for the tobacco, but agreed there was none there. He then seized her and carried her screaming and kicking to a small rear room of the store building where vegetables were kept, she testified. Her description was of an assault only partially completed.*
>
> *The witness said she told Gordon she would have him arrested but that he replied that if she did he would swear against her. She told her mother of the incident when she returned home about an hour later, she said, and shortly accompanied the mother to…where physicians and officers were consulted.*

Although more specifics on this court case were not published in newspaper accounts, the outcome of the trial is known, as follows:

> *Everett Gordon was found not guilty by a jury in superior court…on a charge of criminal assault preferred by his sixteen-year-old sister-in-law. Gordon was indicted by the grand jury on the capital charge but Judge*

McElroy charged the jury that it could return one of two lesser verdicts, assault with intent to rape or assault upon a female, or it might acquit. If there was consent on the part of the prosecuting witness, in the opinion of the jury, this would be ground for acquittal, the court stated.

The jury acquitted Everett Gordon in the assault case.

CHAPTER 2

Amazing and True

Auctioning of Slaves on the Courthouse Steps

The June 11, 1913 edition of the *Dispatch* records reminisces of Uncle George Adams, a former slave, and an alternate view: "Mr. Adams tells that on the first of January of each year, slaves were sold to the highest bidder or rented at the court house, the starting of the event announced by the court house bell. This story is somewhat problematical, as the court house itself didn't have a bell until after 1874."

Slave trade. *Courtesy of the Library of Congress.*

"Auction & Negro Sales." *Courtesy of the Library of Congress.*

According to one historian, this is legend rather than fact:

> *The large blocks on the side of the portico of the Old Court House have been identified in legend and some published works as a site used for auctioning African-American slaves. While there were African-American slaves on the plantations of Davidson County and in several of the larger households, the county never generated sufficient demand for slave labor to make the auctioning of slaves economically practical.*
>
> *There are no records of any slave auctions held in Davidson County at any time, at any place. Rather, slave sales took place between individual slave owners or through itinerant slave dealers who provided slaves "on order."*

WICKED CONTRAST: CHARLIE CHAPLIN'S SERIOUSNESS AND AUDIENCE'S DISAPPOINTMENT

When he appeared on the courthouse steps in April 1918, the excited crowd was expecting the famous silent movie comedian to evoke laughter from his audience. To the disappointment of those present, Chaplin maintained what the anticipating audience deemed wicked seriousness. In his fifteen-minute speech, he urged his audience to buy war bonds during World War I's Third Liberty Loan. Apparently, no comic gestures or antics from the famed Chaplin were on that day's agenda.

Charlie Chaplin. *Courtesy of the Library of Congress.*

The Wednesday, April 27, 1918 edition of the *Dispatch* explored Chaplin's lack of his usual comic self: "There was no hint of the funny walk, the funny mustache and the fancy little tricks that endeared him to every boy's heart in the land in the appearance of Mr. Chaplin here. He favored them only by a funny toss of the hat. When the press asked him to do some funny stunts, he replied, 'It is serious business we are now engaged upon.'"

What Caused the Courthouse Fire of 1865? An Incendiary?

According to Lexington historian J.M. Daniel, natives blamed Union troops:

> *It was generally thought at the time that Union troops had caused the fire, either intentionally or unintentionally. Certainly the use of the court house by the 9th Pennsylvania Cavalry officers during the occupation heightened that impression. Indeed both of the damaged buildings—the court house and Penry's store—had been occupied by Union officers, but it must be again noted that the 9th had been mustered out of service and returned to Harrisburg, Pennsylvania on the 19th of July...several months prior to the fire. Nonetheless, suspicions remained. In February 1866, two months after the fire and long before repairs began, ex-congressman and local lawyer J.M. Leach was authorized by the Court to prepare a memorial and petition to the U.S. Government seeking reimbursement for the repairs.*

Union troops set fire to buildings. *Courtesy of the Library of Congress.*

The Salisbury *Daily Union Banner* published this report in November 1865: "We learn that the fine court house at Lexington, Davidson County, and the building near it, belonging to Mr. Penery [*sic*], were destroyed by fire on Thursday night last. This was doubtless the work of an incendiary."

OLD COURTHOUSE STRANGE TRIAL

Picture the old courthouse in 1921 as described by one historian: "The judge's bench and witness stand look out over an area that was often filled with interested spectators. The bench rail still bears burn marks from ashes from a legion of attorneys' cigarettes and cigars, while the jury boxes still sit on either side of the room."

This was the scene for the 1921 trial for Dr. J.W. Peacock, tried for the murder of Thomasville police chief John Taylor. Historical reports give more details:

> *There was no doubt whatsoever that Peacock had murdered Taylor…it had happened in broad daylight. While the first two shots fired from a second-story window might have been missed by many, there were sufficient*

Stone walls do not a prison make. *Courtesy of the Library of Congress.*

witnesses who saw Dr. Peacock cross the street, pistol in hand, to fire four more shots into a badly wounded and dying Taylor.

All that was in question was whether Dr. Peacock might have been "temporarily insane" due to paranoia brought on by a growing disagreement between the two men.

It appears that each man thought the other was "out to get him." The situation was brought to a crisis point by a mysterious fire in Dr. Peacock's barn. Peacock was convinced that Chief Taylor was the culprit. Even after the shooting the public remained divided in their opinion as to who the real aggrieved party was.

The "temporary insanity" defense wasn't unknown at the time but was unpopular and seldom used, as the corroborating testimony of psychiatrists was less than convincing to a doubting public.

Nonetheless, when the verdict was finally rendered, Dr. Peacock was found innocent due to temporary insanity. He was ordered to the Criminally Insane wing of Raleigh's Central Prison.

All might have ended there as the conclusion of a tragic episode, but the story "grew legs" when Dr. Peacock escaped with the help of a friend, supposedly, in an airplane. He fled to Florida, but facing extradition he again eluded capture, later appearing in California where he would again successfully evade North Carolina's attempts to extradite him. Dr. Peacock died in 1928 in an accident in a California mining camp where he was employed as a medic.

Shabby and Deteriorated Wicked Appearance

From 1855 to 1857, Lexington received rather seething and uncomplimentary comments concerning it shabbiness. For example, the Greensboro *Patriot & Flag* said, "This town is behind many of its sister towns on the road. It has not recently used as much white lead and oil as it might have done to improve its appearance."

The Salisbury *Carolina Watchman* followed by saying:

> *Lexington has deteriorated, at least so far as the eye can enable us to judge….It looks neglected—as if a sort of blight had passed over it. We think it is the worst fenced town we ever saw. The most beautiful yards and lots to be found anywhere in North Carolina are here; but we challenge "log Town" or "Dirt Town" or any other town with any sort of a name to approach Lexington in a comparison of fences.*

FORGERY OF $3.50 CHECK

John Johnstone (aka W.C. Cranford and many other names) was arrested for forgery. The *Dispatch* on August 13, 1936, printed the following report:

> *Two charges of forgery were placed against a man giving his name as John Johnstone, alias W. C. Cranford, alias any number of names, by police who arrested him about 2:30 Tuesday morning. The man had approached Ed. F. Smith at the Smith & Son grocery on East Center Street Monday night about seven and had induced Mr. Smith to cash a check signed with the name of John L. Koonts, local barber shop proprietor in the amount of $3.50. Mr. Smith became suspicious of the check and it proved to be a forgery. He reported to the police department and officers Craver and Goins spotted Johnstone near Michael boarding house on East Second Avenue early Tuesday morning. They called for him to halt, but he fled. Officer Craver gave chase and caught him.*

One might think this one paragraph would be the entire article; however, in 1936, the *Dispatch* was famous for giving "the rest of the story" reproduced below:

> *Investigation of Johnstone's personal belonging proved most interesting to officers. There was another check for $3.50 with the name of Mr. Koonts on it and still another for $3.50 with the name Ed F. Smith & Son Grocery by Gerald F. Smith. Both were forgeries. There were the following signed checks which police believed to be forged. John A. Faucett Grocery, Durham, $5; Owen Printers and Stationers, New Bern, $25; B. E. Baxter, New Bern, $21.35, L.F. Couch, Durham, $3, Independent Oil Company by Luther Whitaker, Durham, $8.50; Friedman's Meat Market, Durham, $7. There were three additional checks, blank, with the name "Owen G. Dunn" written on them and the signature with the name "H.T. Smithers" drawn on the Bank of Wilson.*

Barbershop. *Courtesy of the Library of Congress.*

The saga continues with explicit details:

> *Johnstone had arrived in Lexington and had spent Sunday night at the Carolina Inn, where he had his luggage. Further investigation showed he had a large number of blank checks on various banks, including Durham, Raleigh, Lexington, New Bern, Greensboro, Winston-Salem, Wilson, Lake City, FL and Philadelphia, Pennsylvania. He also had letters of recommendation, which police believe he had written himself. One letter from the Ever Ready Label Corporation, N.Y., discussed a position and a postscript had been added giving Cranford or Johnstone permission to cash check up to $5. This had been added on a different typewriter from the original letter. He also had several different pen points as well as different types of ink. There were a number of order blanks filled out to the Boston Salesbook Co., Boston, Massachusetts, and with each of these orders had a deposit paid attached to the orders were checks signed with the names of the firms supposedly giving the order, for the amount of the deposit. Officers think that the orders were fake and written in order to support the man's tale of the check in order to aid in getting it cashed and that the checks were all forgeries.*

Interrogations by local authorities began immediately; here are the results of the investigation:

> *Chief W.R. Lanning, who did much work on the case, said that the man told him he had been born in Buffalo, served in the Canadian Army during the war and had traveled extensively in this country. He went under the name of Charles H. Johnstone, C.D. Cranford, H.A. Johnstone and others. Among his belongings were many pawn tickets, railroad and bus stubs, notes, names of cities and firms and many other items. There were also some papers belonging to J.N. Ketchie of this city, which Mr. Ketchie said were probably pilfered from his car.*
>
> *Officers said the man was drinking when they arrested him and he was charged with that also. On the two forgery cases he was bound to superior court and bond was set at $500 each by A.J. Newton, judge pro-tem in the absence of Judge Pickard in County Court yesterday morning, when Johnstone waived examination. The drunk charge was continued until August 26. Chief Lanning will make an attempt to investigate the man's career still further before his trial.*

CHILD LABOR IN NOKOMIS COTTON MILL

It is no secret that child labor was not unique in the South, and Nokomis Cotton Mill in Lexington was no exception.

Historians usually agree on the reason for child labor, as explained by the authors of *Like a Family: The Making of a Southern Cotton Mill World*:

> *Reliance on the family labor system meant that the southern textile industry's growth was based to a large extent on the labor of children. Between 1880 and 1910 manufacturers reported that about one-quarter of their work force was under sixteen years of age, and many more child workers went unreported. Indeed, in the industry's early years, youngsters of seven or eight commonly doffed, spun, and did all sorts of casual labor. Originally the official definition of "children" applied to youngsters up to age eight but later rose to age twelve, then fourteen, and finally sixteen; nevertheless, young people remained crucial, both to the industry's profit margins and to their own families' survival.*

Above: Workers in the Nokomis Cotton Mill, Lexington, North Carolina. *Courtesy of the Library of Congress.*

Left: The smallest boy at Nokomis Cotton Mill said he was eleven years old and made fifty cents a day. *Courtesy of the Library of Congress.*

President Woodrow Wilson, with his wife standing at his side. *Courtesy of the Library of Congress.*

In 1916 President Woodrow Wilson signed the Keating-Owen Child Labor bill that stopped the employment of children in cotton mills. Possibly the impetuous for this bill came from Lewis Hine's photographs of children:

Given the inadequacy of state legislation, members of the NCLC felt the need for federal action. To mobilize public opinion against child labor, the NCLC devised a highly effective propaganda campaign. Key to this effort were the photographs of Lewis Hine, which poignantly revealed the youthfulness of southern workers. Hine's images—of little girls dressed in long skirts and aprons and little boys wearing their workingmen's caps and suspenders, all swallowed up in rows of towering machines—became the crusade's symbols of the worst evils of industrialization. The NCLC convinced the public and members of Congress that the employment of children had to be stopped.

In the following article, the *Dispatch* of August 19, 1936, reminded Lexington employers that children younger than sixteen must have work permits:

Welfare officer Curry F. Lopp states that the report has come to him that a number of business houses in Lexington...are employing children under 16 years of age, who do not have work card permits. All children under l6 who engage in any kind of work, must, under the law have one of the cards, which will be issued after they have come to the welfare office here, secured blanks and properly filled these out. The law provides a fine and penalty for employers working children without cards.

CHAPTER 3

Front-Page Sensationalism

MURDERED BY DUDLEY MOORE

Victoria Catherine Corilla Tussey ("Vic") born January 13, 1872, married Jacob Gordon Berrier in 1892. She died on 15 Aug. 1931 at age 59, murdered by Dudley Moore. Her body was interred in Aug 1931 at Davidson County, NC. Beulah United Church of Christ Cemetery, on Arnold Road.

Those are the statistics. The following are the gory details from the Wednesday, August 13, 1936 *Dispatch*:

"MOTIVE REVEALED; MURDER GUN FOUND: Negro Suspect In Berrier Murder Rushed to Jail Outside of This County"
MOTIVE
Criminal assault was in all likelihood the motive that prompted the slaying of Mrs. Jacob G. Berrier, 59, in an upstairs room in her home Saturday afternoon.

The Dispatch *IS JUST NOW AT LIBERTY TO REVEAL INFORMATION FURNISHED IT LAST MIDNIGHT FROM OFFICIAL SOURCES, BUT WHICH INFORMATION WAS GIVEN UNDER PLEDGE OF THE STRICTEST SILENCE UNTIL THE HOUR ARRIVED WHEN IT MIGHT BE REVEALED. THAT HOUR HAS ARRIVED.*

It is learned that definite evidence to this effect was discovered some several hours after the slaying and that at least four persons are in position to give rather conclusive testimony as to this.

Before leaving for Chapel Hill this morning, Sheriff James A. Leonard sanctioned publication of this information under certain specified conditions. Since the first extra edition went to press the paper has been able to meet the condition imposed.

Details as to this evidence are here withheld, but they are known to be in possession of Sheriff Leonard and a very few others, who likewise have kept this matter under cover for good reason.

The front page of the *Dispatch* on Wednesday, August 13, 1936, revealed not only the above "Motive Revealed" article, but triple headlines including the following:

"BLOOD ANALYSIS IS BEING MADE AT CHAPEL HILL: SHIRT FOUND LAST NIGHT PROVES THE LEAD SOUGHT
"MOORE CONTENDS HE IS INNOCENT
"STORIES TOLD ABOUT HIS MOVEMENTS SATURDAY FOUND FALSE"

The shotgun with which Mrs. Jacob G. Berrier was beaten and shot to death in her home Saturday afternoon was found in a clump of honeysuckle vines about 200 yards southwest of the home at ll:45 today. Fred Wilson and Ham Berrier, neighbors, found the gun.

The weapon was in four pieces, having been taken apart, but still contained the empty shell. Some blood is on the weapon and the stock is splintered. One piece of the stock is believed to be good fingerprints. There was also a small piece of Mrs. Berrier's dress sticking to a portion of the gun.

The long sought weapon was rushed to Winston-Salem to be examined by fingerprint experts and any prints secured will immediately be compared with the finger prints of Dudley Moore, 18-year-old negro, who lived at the Berrier home and who was arrested last night and rushed to a jail outside the county for safekeeping during further investigation.

Hundreds joined this morning in search for the gun after clothing of Moore; especially a shirt newly discovered, was seized last night and held for examination of stains apparently those of blood. Other circumstances pointing to the probable guilt of Moore added impetus to the search as it was believed to be at no great distance from the home.

A number of people had been near the spot where the gun was found, but the honeysuckle thicket was a very dense one. A newspaper man

Honeysuckle. *Courtesy of the Library of Congress.*

> *walked several feet into the vines on Sunday morning, but despaired at trying to penetrate further.*

The following contradictions abounded in stories told by Dudley Moore, the eighteen-year-old Negro whom Mr. and Mrs. Berrier had befriended since his childhood:

> *L. Blaylock and Sam Berrier discovered a blue work shirt later acknowledged by the suspect as his, lying in a woodshed near where Moore had placed other articles to soak in a washtub. The sleeves of the shirt were rolled up and at first it did not appear stained, but when these were unrolled, it was stated, decided stains appearing to be blood, were found on the lower sleeves.*

A TRUE STORY ABOUT MEN KILLING EACH OTHER

Joe Sink, retired publisher of the Lexington *Dispatch*, graciously shared with me the talk he gave to the O. Henry Study Club of Lexington. His topic was "Men Killing Each Other," and since his voice and tone are unsurpassed in true southern storytelling, his presentation is included here in its entirety:

> *You probably have heard stories about some of these things and certainly about many of the people involved, especially if you're from Lexington. But while some of what you've heard may have bordered on the truth, I'm going to give you the real thing from the pages of The* Dispatch *way back when newspapers printed just about anything that was local.*
>
> *This is really two separate stories tied into one, with one man playing a leading role in both events. And while they took place 37 years apart, they happened only five blocks away from each other on Main Street here in Lexington.*
>
> *The man in both stories is, as some of you would know, Baxter Shemwell. He was 37 when the first incident occurred, and 74 at the time of the second.*
>
> *Baxter Shemwell was the son of a prominent Tyro doctor named O.M. Shemwell and Sally Thomason Shemwell, who was the sister of the Mrs. Hargrave who was Ham Hargrave's mother and Bill Gordon Wrights' grandmother. Baxter was the oldest of 13 children, and one of the newspaper articles I read described him as a small, wiry man with a "jumpy step."*
>
> *Among his 12 brothers and sisters was Mrs. W.J. Vestal, whose home was on West First Avenue on what's now the side yard of Kathy and Cloyd Philpott, right beside Daniel and Ashley Timberlake's house. I actually knew Mrs. Vestal when I was six or seven years old and living on First Avenue, but I never knew any of the others.*
>
> *Baxter lived in Lexington in his early life, doing well for himself. He became quite wealthy, and he was the president of Lexington Drug Co. He also owned other businesses and later he was involved in an enterprise called "The Wizard Automobile Company of Charlotte," which reportedly sold a great deal of stock but never produced an automobile.*
>
> *Later though, in the latter part of my story, he had more or less been banished from Lexington because, in part of the first incident I'm going to tell you about, and in part because of other misdeeds, and by that time he was living in Asheville.*

But to start at the beginning of this story as I'm telling it, you go back all the way to February 25, 1895, when Baxter was 37 years old.

On that day Baxter was involved in a dispute with a local physician, Dr. R.L. Payne, and his son, R.L. Payne, Jr., also a doctor. Some of you may recognize the name of Dr. Payne because of his gravestone that you can see in the city cemetery with the inscription "Assassinated February 25, 1895." It's a large stone right beside the road through the cemetery that's closest to Center Street when you come up the hill from Salem Street to State Street.

So on that February Monday, Mr. Shemwell, according to The Dispatch*'s coverage of the event, was mad at the younger Dr. Payne over some kind of insurance policy, taken out by Mr. Shemwell on Dr. Payne's advice.*

There had been "sharp words," the paper reported, between the two at a barber shop on Saturday night, and then on Monday Mr. Shemwell went by the office of the doctors, where the first trouble occurred and where, it was reported, shots were fired. But no one was harmed.

Shortly after that, though, Mr. Shemwell was seen walking up and down Main Street with a shotgun on his shoulder.

Someone got word of this to Mrs. Shemwell, and she arrived at the scene and "begged and pleaded," with her husband, the paper said, and he went back to his Lexington Drug Company location.

Then, still later that same morning, because of the altercation and the gunshots, Mr. Shemwell and both of the doctors were brought before a justice of the peace, who ordered them to make an appearance in court and released them under $200 bonds.

After posting his bond, Shemwell went back by the drug store and told what was referred to as "a crowd of people there" that he was going. His home was on South Main Street a short distance below the office of the doctors, apparently somewhere below the present Civic Center across the street from the Presbyterian Church.

Well, it turned out that Shemwell began his walk somewhat behind the Paynes, who had already started down Main Street and who had a small crowd accompanying them. There was another group with Mr. Shemwell, and at some point somebody looked back from the first group and said, "Look out, Doctor, Baxter Shemwell is coming."

The newspaper account then said there was some crowd confusion, but Baxter Shemwell, on catching up with the Paynes, took out a large "Colt's pistol," and fired into Dr. Payne's chest. That was Dr. Payne, Sr.

As Dr. Payne fell, the paper said, he clutched at Mr. Shemwell and they both fell from the sidewalk into the street. This was described during the trial by Dr. Payne, Jr. as being "nearly opposite the Presbyterian Church," and very close to Dr. Payne's office. It was also close to the Shemwell home, a little farther south on Main Street.

Shemwell was then grabbed by officers and taken away. But Dr. Payne was beyond help. He was "tenderly carried" to his nearby residence, the paper said, and after about 20 to 25 minutes he "expired," quoting again.

This was when newspapers wrote things much differently than they do today, which probably was a good idea, and at this point The Dispatch *article read, "Ah, what a spectacle to bring the hardest heart to feelings of emotions when Mrs. Shemwell and little son Dermot followed the husband and father to his cell"*

"But Ah, on the other hand, what must have been the feelings of the family of Dr. Payne when they surveyed the husband and father cold in death."

The article continued by saying that Mr. Shemwell "avers" that he did the killing in self-defense. And the paper said there was much sympathy for families on either side.

So, over four months later, on July 4, 1895, the trial began. The names of 300 men-women being "too emotional and not considered to be sound enough thinkers to decide important matters were therefore not eligible to serve on juries" the paper said—were drawn from the jury box and the entire first day was spent selecting the jury.

And imagine this: Mr. Shemwell's attorneys were the Honorable C.B. Watson of Winston, the Honorable R.Z. Linney of Taylorsville, Robbins and Raper of Lexington, and Pickens and Walser of Lexington. That's serious business there. Remember I mentioned earlier he was quite wealthy. Enough to hire six lawyers.

So then, after much testimony and 421 hours of deliberation, and despite testimony by Dr. Payne, Jr. that Baxter Shemwell had two pistols, one pointed at him and one at his father, the jury went along with Baxter Shemwell's plea of self-defense and the six attorneys arguing it for him, and found him not guilty. And so ended the Dr. Payne episode..

And by the way there still is a baptismal font in the Presbyterian Church honoring Dr. Payne, a ruling elder from 1859 to 1895, and just 61 years old when he died.

Joe Sink's talk to the O. Henry Study Club does not end here. Fast forward thirty-seven years for the rest of the saga:

The next incident I'll talk about, and the final incident for Mr. Shemwell, happened 37 years after the Payne shooting. Shemwell was 74 years old by then, but it's certain the time hadn't mellowed him as, according to the newspaper account "he had many run-ins and used a gun a number of times, this perhaps being the seventh."

During that intervening 37 years, one of the things you may know about Baxter Shemwell occurred, and that is how the road from Lexington to Denton going by Central High School, which is officially Highway 47, came to be called the Shemwell Highway. You might know it's called that because Mr. Shemwell spent some of the time between the fatal gunfights working on that road as a prisoner. You may know that, but you probably don't know what got him his prison time.

What led to that sentence was a strange incident here in Lexington involving Wade Phillips and John Bower, two attorneys I knew when I started work at The Dispatch *in 1958.*

That incident was a run-in that took place in the law office of the two men, when Shemwell appeared one day, quote, "with two drawn .45s," angry because the attorneys had refused to accept a retainer from him and declined to represent him in whatever matter it was that he was concerned about at the time. Shooting broke out. Baxter fired one shot that went through Major Phillips' coat, and then Mr. Bower, who at this time was the district attorney, knocked him unconscious with a paper clamp, one of those heavy things lawyers used to put seals on legal documents.

Shemwell was arrested and convicted of assault, and given a sentence of 30 months on the chain gang. However, before he could be taken away he ran, and remained at large for several months. Although he was declared an outlaw, he made several appearances here and in Salisbury before he was arrested over there by the sheriff and sent to the road gang.

And it was during the time he was serving that sentence, working on the highway, that he got a road named for himself.

After that, at some point Mr. Shemwell moved to Asheville.

The next part of Joe Sink's presentation to the O. Henry Study Club is informative and poignant and takes current Lexingtonians back to their hometown as it was long ago:

But in May, 1932, he came back to Lexington to see Adam L. Sink, who was a resident of North Main Street, living where the BB&T office is now and who was the owner of a grocery store where Noah's restaurant is, across Main Street from the police department. He was also a relative of mine, or at least my grandfather's.

In reading about this I got interested in what uptown Lexington would have been like in 1932 so I made a list of the Main Street stores between Court Square and Second Street, just to give you an idea of what was there.

Beginning at Center Street and going north on the east side of Main, across the street from Conrad and Hinkle, you would have passed, in the two blocks before you got to Second Street, Cy's Coffee shop, coincidentally right where the Perfect Blend coffee shop is now, the A&P, Hanes One-Two-Three Store, Koonts Barber Shop, J. F. Wards, the Commercial and Savings Bank, Lexington Hardware, Miller's Studio. Then across First Street to Kirkman and Penninger Furniture, Beeson's Flower Shop, Hege Brothers Grocers, J.K. Hawkins General Merchandise, A.L. Sink Grocery which as I said was where Noah's Restaurant is now, Piedmont Furniture, and a boarding house occupied by W.C. Russell and, I'm told, Lexington's first Chinaman, Hong Loo. No kidding

Okay. That was just a little sidebar of information.

So, in 1932, as I said, Baxter came back to Lexington mad at Adam Sink apparently because of financial problems. He owed Mr. Sink $100,000, and the newspaper accounts implied that foreclosure proceedings had been started against the Shemwell home in Asheville on Merrimon Avenue, and Mr. Shemwell wanted the proceedings to be withdrawn. The depression had set in and was in full swing, and financial ruin loomed.

The Asheville residence was said to be a $50,000 house, and that would have been huge in 1932. I mentioned earlier that Shemwell was president, years before, of Lexington Drug Co., and at the time of this last incident he also owned a farm implement business and a stable, along with the drug store. But as I said, the depression was here, and financial problems with it.

Anyway, he had a chauffeur drive him to Lexington on May 30, arriving late at night, and he got a room at the March Hotel. And on May 31, 1932, he decided to have it out with Mr. Sink.

So he went to the Main Street grocery store where bad timing caught up with him.

When he walked into the store, Mr. Sink was, quote, "weighing up a pound of coffee for a Mr. Tussy with his back toward the door when Mr. Shemwell entered and announced he had come for a settlement."

Continuing the newspaper account, "Almost at this moment Mr. Sink's two sons-in-law entered the front door." The sons-in-law were Jerry

Boaze, who many of you remember and who was married to Mary Sink and who owned Boaze Motor Co., and Dr. F.G. Johnson, also remembered by some of you, who was a dentist and married to Louise Sink. It's also in my memory that Dr. Johnson owned the Lexington minor league baseball team in about 1950. Well, Mr. Boaze and Dr. Johnson were aware that Shermwell was in town and they had come to the store armed to defend Mr. Sink if necessary.

And it was necessary, of course. The article continued "So Shemwell, it was stated, reached for an automatic pistol he carried in his pocket, but Boaze beat him to the draw, whereupon Shemwell threw up his hands."

Johnson then took hold of Shemwell while Boaze removed the pistol and escorted him outside to his waiting car.

Shemwell's driver, who had stayed with the car, then drove off but stopped less than a block away and turned and came back. He stopped again, across the street from the grocery store, and Shemwell got out again with a rifle in his hands.

Boaze, who had gone outside when Shemwell was leaving, had remained on the sidewalk, and as Shemwell stepped behind a car and began firing the rifle, Boaze returned fire with his own automatic pistol. And Dr. Johnson also began firing from the door of the grocery store.

The paper said about 15 shots were fired, hitting cars and windows, before Police Chief Bruce Talbert crept up behind Shemwell, hit him in the head with his pistol, and grabbed him.

Chief Talbert at first didn't think anyone was wounded, but he discovered that Shemwell had been hit in the side with what proved to be the fatal wound. Initially it wasn't known whether Jerry Boaze or Dr. Johnson fired the shot, but it turnout out to be from a .32 caliber pistol fired by Jerry Boaze.

Shemwell then was taken to the Davidson Hospital, located at the corner of North Main and West Fourth Street where Char's is now, with the wound in his abdomen. He died shortly after 10 o'clock that night.

On Thursday, June 2, a funeral service for Mr. Shemwell was held at the home of Dr. W.J. Vestal on First Avenue. Dr. Vestal was married to Shemwell's sister, as I said earlier. Rev. J.M. Hayes of the First Baptist Church officiated. The remains were taken to Tyro and laid to rest, The Dispatch *said, in the Shemwell's private cemetery just off Michael Road in Tyro. The cemetery is just 100 yards or so from Highway 150 and it's where the parents of the deceased and other near relatives were buried. Baxter is in an unmarked grave in the little fenced-in cemetery, now overgrown with small trees.*

When he died he was 74 years old, and eight of his 12 brothers and sisters, all younger than he as he was the eldest of 13 children, had preceded him in death. Three sisters, Mrs. Vestal, one living in Richmond and one in Asheville, and a brother in Richmond were still alive.

The newspaper obituary said Shemwell was descended from pioneer forbearers of this county on both sides. It added that the original Shemwell of the group settled in what is now Jackson Hill township in 1740.

Baxter Shemwell was first married to Laura Bernheim, daughter of "widely known," it said, R.L. Bernheim, a Lutheran minister who for a time was pastor of St. Luke's and Pilgrim churches in Davidson County. Miss Bernheim, or Mrs. Shemwell, was the mother of Dermont Shemwell of Albany, and was Mary Phillips' grandmother.

His second marriage was to a Mrs. Sue Harman, who died well before this time, and they had a son, Everard B. Shemwell, whom the paper said was a student at the University of North Carolina at the time of this occurrence.

The funeral on June 2, by the way, was conducted by Kirkman & Son Funeral Home, which now is Davidson Funeral Home. Jack Briggs found the receipt for the service for me, and the whole thing cost $280. Jack was checking to see if they still owed anything, and thought I might like a copy of the receipt.

Going back a little bit now, to the day before the funeral, on June 1, a coroner's jury was convened, made up of six men, for the purpose of determining whether any criminal charges should be brought for the fatal shooting.

- *Members of the jury were Ed. F. Smith, who had an insurance business on East Center Street on the left just after you cross the railroad bridge, and who also lived at the same location and was the father of Gerald Smith who later had a grocery store on that location; and*
- *E.B. Craven of West Third Avenue, Dr. Jean's father-in-law and Scott Craven's grandfather, who was at that time manager of the insurance department at Commercial and Savings Bank and vice president of Dixie Furniture; and*
- *C.L. Davis of Hargrave Street, secretary-treasurer of Davidson Motor Co. and certainly likely a member of Lonnie Davis' family; and*
- *C.R. Wagner of 15 Vance Circle, president of Leonard and Wagner Tire Co. and certainly likely a member of Big Wag and Little Wag's family; and*

- *C.M. Ward of 410 North Salisbury Street, building contractor and the Ward of Ward Lumber Co. so definitely a member of the Gayle Ward Burke and Chip Ward family; and*
- *Roby G. Loflin, the Davidson County jailer who lived at the jail at 115 North Salisbury Street.*

> *In a very short hearing, Mr. Boaze and Dr. Johnson said their act was in self-defense and justifiable and that they were blameless, and the jury quickly acquitted them. So that ended the life and the gun slinging Shemwell career.*

At this point in his presentation, Joe Sink paused. Then he told his captive audience this was not quite the end of the story. Since this was the O. Henry Study Club he was speaking to, and since one of the things people liked about O. Henry were his surprise off-beat endings, he now had one to relate:

> *Way back on July 7, 1881, 13 years before the Payne shooting and 50 years before Shemwell died, The* Dispatch *had a big story. The paper at that time was almost brand new, only two months and two days old. And in case you didn't know, it's the oldest business in Lexington now by a good margin. In 1881 it was owned by the founder, W.B. Eldridge, and it would be three more years before my Grandfather Fred O. Sink, Sr. started working there. So this old story was about, you guessed it, Baxter Shemwell and guns.*
>
> *Mr. Shemwell, who would have been 24 at the time, got into a gunfight on the street with a Mr. Charles M. Thompson.*
>
> *They met at the front door of C.F. Lowe's store, which I was told was on the square, and drew pistols and opened fire. Thompson was not hit, but Shemwell was shot four times. The paper said "One bullet passed through his body, one lodged in a lung, one hit his right arm and the fourth hit his thigh.*
>
> *The article continued, "Shemwell was removed to his home and was thought to be in a dying condition, but at this time he still lives and may recover, through that is improbable."*
>
> *But, as you now know, he did, of course, recover from that incident, thanks to the skillful care of his physician, whom you remember from earlier in this story, Dr. R.L. Payne.*

"THAT MAN AIN'T AFRAID OF THE DEVIL"

Making the front page of the October 10, 1905 *Dispatch* was an article entitled, "Negro Made Threats: Said He Would Kill White Boss and Then Fled and Was Taken After Hot Chase." The following is the newspaper account of what happened:

> *There was an exciting incident here in town Monday that, following on the heels of the murder Sunday, sent flagging interest up several notches. One of the negroes who worked on the railroad was in town with two companions and was making open threats as to what he was going to do with Mr. Butler, one of the foremen at a camp near town. He asserted that he was going to kill him on the first opportunity.*
>
> *Mr. Butler was in town at the time and hearing of the negro's threats, went after him. He found him at the corner of Main and Depot streets and when he started to dismount, the negro ran. He came up Main, went down First Avenue and crossing between Mr. W.C.B. Leonard's and Mr. E.E. Raper's houses, went on back of the graded school, then up Sixth Avenue into Mr. D.F. Conrad's back yard. He had a good start of the officers that went after him, and might have escaped had he run fast enough. Instead of running faster he went into Mr. Conrad's house, telling Mrs. Conrad that he wished to hide. The lady was frightened and naturally made no protest. He went right up the stairs into a room and hid behind a door.*
>
> *Bob Heitman and Raymond Dorsett found him and drawing their guns, made him stick up his hands with neatness and dispatch. He was searched, nothing being found, and brought up for trial. A large crowd followed him and the courthouse was choked with people when he was tried. He was fined $50 in one case, trespass, and $10 and costs for disturbing the peace, or sixty days on the roads. To the roads he went.*
>
> *Nothing was made out of his threats against Mr. Butler, who laughed at the idea of a peace bond. "To have placed him under such a bond," said one, "Mr. Butler would have had to swear that he was afraid of the nigger, and that man ain't afraid of the devil!"*

WOMAN BRUTALLY MURDERED

The *Dispatch* headlines on Monday, August 13, 1951, read "WOMAN BRUTALLY MURDERED: Battered Body Found in Hall Main St. Home. Mrs.

H.W. Hinshaw, 65, Member Of Prominent Family, Is Victim of Vicious Killer; Struggle Evident." The article following those headlines is this:

> *One of the most brutal murders ever committed in Davidson County was discovered shortly before nine o'clock this morning when the body of Mrs. Beulah Miller Hinshaw, 65, widow of H.W. Hinshaw was found in the back hall of her home at 950 South Main Street.*
>
> *The body, apparently almost completely stripped of clothing in what had evidently been a terrific struggle, was found just inside the back hall-door, wrapped in a bedspread that had evidently been taken from Mrs. Hinshaw's bedroom nearby. The body lay near an open trunk from which books, papers and other articles had evidently been piled on the floor, and part of the body lay across these articles, indicating the trunk had been entered before the body was placed there.*
>
> *Dr. David E. Plummer, County coroner, arriving here from Thomasville about 11:40 ordered the body taken to Davidson Funeral Home. He said he would continue his investigation of the case there.*
>
> *Dr. Plummer, upon early examination of the remains, said death apparently came from a stab wound in the left chest. He said the wound probably penetrated the heart but that closer examination would be necessary before any definite decision was reached.*

Tuesday, August 14, 1951 edition of the local newspaper had glaring headlines: "NEGRO HELD IN HINSHAW MURDER. Suspect Is Questioned In Brutal Murder and Rape; Name Withheld By Police." Although the suspect's name was "withheld," this appeared beneath the larger headlines: "Unofficially Identified as John Roman, Ice Plant Worker; Suspect Kept in Winston-Salem Overnight," with the following story:

> *Police Chief V.G. Price stated shortly after noon today that the police department is holding a Negro man, a suspect for questioning in the slaying of Mrs. Beaulah Miller Hinshaw, local widow.*
>
> *Chief Price added that police are running down all clues they could find in the case as well as clues furnished to the department.*
>
> *The Negro man was not identified but Chief Price said he was being questioned.*
>
> *Unofficial reports, not released by police, are that the Negro's name is John Roman, father of four children and a veteran of World War II. Roman's home address is listed on East Third Avenue and he has been working at a local ice plant.*

> *It was also unofficially learned that the suspect was taken to Winston-Salem last night for safe-keeping and was returned to this city this morning.*

A separate article on page one of the Tuesday newspaper carried this headline: "Coroner Says Mrs. Hinshaw Was Raped":

> *An autopsy report, released this morning by Dr. David F. Plummer, Davidson County coroner, reveals that Mrs. Beulah Miller Hinshaw, 65-year-old "local widow was both criminally assaulted and murdered at her home on South Main Street here late Sunday evening.*
>
> *The report, completed early this morning, after extensive study by Dr. Plummer and an expert pathologist from Greensboro, reveals the beloved Lexington woman met her death at the hands of a person or persons unknown.*
>
> *Mrs. Hinshaw, whose battered remains were found by her sister and a neighbor at the Hinshaw home about 9 o'clock yesterday morning, died of a stab wound in the chest or a fracture or dislocation of the neck, or both, according to Dr. Plummer.*
>
> *First reports were that death probably came from a stab wound in the left chest, but complete autopsy conducted last night revealed the fractured or dislocated neck. X-ray pictures were scheduled to be made today to determine the injury.*
>
> *The autopsy also indicated that Mrs. Hinshaw was criminally assaulted, Dr. Plummer points out. He stated the woman was probably attacked and killed roughly between 10 to 15 hours before the time her body was found yesterday morning. This would set the death late Sunday night, probably around 11 o'clock.*
>
> *Specimens taken during the autopsy, finally completed this morning, will be studied for further clues, Dr. Plummer said. He indicated that further tests would include laboratory study.*
>
> *In speaking of the slash wound, found in the left chest, Dr. Plummer said it was inflected by a sharp instrument but that neither the heart nor great vessels of the body had been struck or penetrated. He said the deceased could have suffered great shock due to the stab, thus causing death. He said a person of Mrs. Hinshaw's age could go into shock quite easily, and added that evidence of a struggle found at the rear of the home indicated the woman had fought her murderer. He also stated that there were signs of hemorrhage around the wound.*
>
> *Scratches and bruises about the face were also found as the remains were examined at the Davidson Funeral Home here. Dr. Plummer also added that markings about the neck indicated strangulation.*

Dr. Plummer said he had reached the conclusion that Mrs. Hinshaw had been attacked and murdered and that no coroner's jury would have to be summoned.

A photograph in Tuesday's newspaper had the heading "Grim Scene Shows Body of Slain Woman," and the caption reads, "The body of the raped, murdered 65-year-old woman is shown wrapped in a bedspread."

Wednesday's front page carried large, bold headlines, "NEGRO CONTINUES TO DENY MURDER," accompanied by a small headline entitled, "Coroner Makes Further Report: Questioning of Suspect Continues; SBI Making Additional Lab Tests." The lengthy but interesting newspaper story follows:

Police continued to probe into the murder-criminal attack case of Mrs. Beulah Miller Hinshaw here today and John Roman, 29-year old Negro suspect was scheduled for more questioning.

Roman spent last night in Davidson County jail and will face more questioning today. He has reportedly continued to deny he knows anything about the case.

In the meantime police are studying various clues—a footprint found near the murder scene, tire-tracks apparently from a truck that Roman might have had access to, a low cut rubber boot found near the murder scene, and others.

This morning Dr. David E. Plummer, county coroner, who along with a pathologist conducted an autopsy on Mrs. Hinshaw's body, stated it was indicated a knife was used to slash the small widow victim in the left chest and slash her about the throat. Prior to this time Dr. Plummer had stated a sharp instrument was used to make the wounds.

Dr. Plummer also stated that closer study of specimens taken from the body definitely indicated that criminal assault had been attempted but that study of the specimens could not definitely confirm that criminal assault had been completed.

The coroner also added that X-ray examinations taken yesterday slowed four broken ribs and another that had been cracked. He said these injuries were probably caused by someone grabbing the woman and crushing her. He said ribs of a woman of Mrs. Hinshaw's age were usually brittle and could be crushed more easily than a younger person. The victim was 65 years of age at the time of her death.

Dr. Plummer stated that X-Ray pictures located an apparent fracture of the neck. Study of the body prior to X-rays indicated a dislocation and apparent fracture of the neck, he said.

Scrapings from beneath the fingernails of the victim have been reportedly turned over to the SBI for laboratory study. These scraping could add considerably to the case, should anything be found. If the deceased scratched her murderer particles of skin might be located beneath the fingernails.

Dr. Plummer added that cries attempted by the victim could easily have been muffled, after careful study of the body. Strangulation would have checked such cries so they could not have been heard very far. He also said Mrs. Hinshaw could have been so badly frightened she might not have been able to cry out.

The coroner said yesterday that death was caused by stab wounds or dislocation or fracture of the neck or both. He also stated that the woman could have gone into shock at the time of the attack and that such shock at her age could cause death.

Absence of any considerable amount of blood either in the Hinshaw home on South Main Street or in the backyard where a struggle was indicated, suggested the deceased could have bled internally or that two rainstorms Sunday night might have washed blood into the ground. One splotch of blood was found in the house where the near-nude body was located Monday morning, wrapped in a pink bedspread. A beaten down area of grass at the rear of the house indicated a struggle had taken place, but no large amount of blood was noted. The rain might have washed this away. Torn articles of clothing, one of them spotted with blood, were found at this scene.

Thursday, August 16, 1951, had huge bold letters proclaiming: "ROMAN CHARGED. Police Swear Out Warrant for Murder Against Suspected Negro. Fingerprints at Hinshaw Home March Those of Charged Man. Arrested Is Moved from County Jail for Safekeeping by Local Police." This story follows:

A warrant, charging John Andrew Roman, local Negro with the murder of Mrs. Beulah Miller Hinshaw, 65-year old Lexington widow, late Sunday night, was sworn out today by Chief V.G. Price.

Chief Price, making a public statement in the case, said charges against Roman were official today. The Negro ice plant worker has been a suspect since Monday when he was picked up by police for questioning.

In making his statement to The Dispatch *THIS MORNING, Chief Price said he had kept the whereabouts of Roman secret due to the fact that he had received unidentified telephone calls threatening to do bodily harm to Roman. He did not elaborate on this statement.*

Actual whereabouts of the Negro was not made public this morning. Roman did spend the night in Davidson County jail Tuesday night after it was announced a Negro suspect was being held, but he was not in jail here Monday night or last night.

> **Fingerprints Match.** *Chief Price in his statements this morning said fingerprints found in the Hinshaw house and processed by Lou Williams, SBI agent, and H.W. Zimmerman, Lexington's city manager and former SBI and FBI agent, both fingerprint experts, were identified by SBI laboratories in Raleigh as those of Roman.*
>
> **Stolen Articles Found.** *Yesterday afternoon about four o'clock, more clues in the case were found in a building across the street from the ice plant where Roman was employed prior to his apprehension by police.*
>
> *The latest clues were a pistol and two watches allegedly owned by the victim and missing from her house since the time of her death.*
>
> *The .38 caliber pistol, one Mrs. Hinshaw kept in a drawer of her bedroom, her own watch and a pocket watch of her late husband, H.W. Hinshaw, that the victim carried with her, were found in a one story brick building directly in front of the local ice plant, which was originally used as a creamery.*
>
> *Workers removing a large walk-in cooler which had been stored in the building, reportedly found the watches. The manager of the plant reportedly heard of the discovery and called the police. The manager reportedly later found the gun, wrapped in a gunny-sack hidden in the attic above. All the items were turned over to police.*
>
> *Roman was employed at the ice plant on the night shift as an ice puller. It was stated in The* Dispatch *yesterday from a reliable source that his duties were at the plant and not away from it. His only work with the public was delivery of ice on the plant platform to customers that might visit the plant for it.*
>
> *Roman's age is not officially known, but Chief Price said his wife said he was 28. He is a father of four small children, the oldest about seven years of age. He is a veteran of World War II, is listed to weigh 171 pounds, and is six feet, two inches tall.*
>
> *He came to Lexington from South Carolina for the first time before World War II and worked at the local ice plant. He later entered the army and returned here after his discharge about three and one-half years ago.*

A newspaper article prepared as a Turn Back the Clock column, but never published, summarizes the court trial, verdict and sentencing:

> *Roman's trial began Monday, Jan. 28, 1952, in Davidson County Superior Court. Roman, who was black, was represented by two black lawyers from Winston-Salem, Hosea Price and Harold Epps. Charles Hagan, the solicitor for Davidson County, represented the state.*

Price presented a motion to have the grand jury indictment for first-degree murder dismissed. He claimed blacks had been deliberately excluded from the grand jury, but Judge Will Pless Jr. denied the motion and noted that three of the 18 members of the grand jury were black.

Due to the publicity about the case, 48 potential jurors were brought in from Guilford County, including 15 blacks, in accordance with a motion made by Price. Four black jurors were seated on the jury Tuesday.

The state presented its evidence throughout Wednesday. In addition to detailing Roman's actions the night of the murder, they also presented several pieces of circumstantial evidence linking Roman to the death of Hinshaw, who was white. In addition to the items found in the building across from the ice plant, fingerprints found on a metal box in the house matched Roman's. Also, hairs on a rubber boot found in Hinshaw's yard matched hair samples from Roman's leg.

"The courtroom was crowded all the time," Parks said. "A lot of the public didn't understand the scientific part of it. There were no outbursts. It was very emotional, considering the lady she was, and the conditions (of the murder)."

The state rested its case Thursday, and the defense presented no evidence. Parks said Price and Epps were counting on the jurors not convicting Roman based on circumstantial evidence. Jurors deliberated until 9 P.M. Thursday, and returned a guilty verdict on Friday. State law required Roman be sentenced to death, and an execution date was set for March 21, 1952, in the state penitentiary in Raleigh.

Parks noted the case was the first time in Davidson County a man had been convicted solely on circumstantial evidence.

Roman appealed his conviction to the state Supreme Court, but the appeal was denied. He was asphyxiated with cyanide gas on Friday, June 6, 1952. According to court records, the following people witnessed the execution: Parks, J.E. Thompson, Fletcher Foard, Lawrence Byerly, Robert W. Bowers and Wade H. Phillips, along with the warden and physician of the penitentiary. Parks said Cletus McCrary, Clarence Cook and Ed Weisner, Lexington police officers, also made the trip to Raleigh.

"I observed the multiple conditions of the deceased (Hinshaw), and it was actually an ease of mind to see him put away," Parks said.

Author's note: We lived not too many blocks away from Mrs. Hinshaw, and that was the first time in my life I had been frightened. I would not allow my parents to open my bedroom windows at night. They must have also been just a little afraid as well, because that was the first time we ever locked our front door at night.

CHAPTER 4

Believe It or Not

White Slave Trading

On July 5, 1911, the *Dispatch* printed the following article entitled, "An Ugly-Looking Case Close to Home: Trial Postponed Until Monday Afternoon at Four":

> *There is an ugly case scheduled for Monday afternoon at four o'clock before Mayor Moyer in which the state of North Carolina is plaintiff and Charles Noel and his wife, Jamie Noel, nee Jamie Wolf, are defendants. Those who read the papers carefully have heard frequently of the so-called "white slave" cases in New York, Chicago and other wicked centers and many a man's blood has boiled with indignation as he read. This case comes close home and has some ugly phases. It may not be a case of "white slave traffic," but it looks very much like it. The story is substantially as follows:*
>
> *Along about the first of May Noel's wife, who was Jamie Wolf, came to Lexington to visit her mother and other relatives here. Her husband came here once or twice during her visit, and he was here on the day that the abduction took place. From what can be learned about it, this was engineered by the woman. It is alleged that she approached several young girls and tried to lure them away from home with the promise of fine clothes, easy money and a good time. Clara Beil Gibbs daughter of Mr. H.E. Gibbs, of the Dacotah Cotton Mill, and Vertie Kinley, daughter of Mr. Robert Kinley of the Wennonah, fell for her line of talk and consented to go with her. Neither of the children knew that the other was going until*

they met at the station. They slipped away from their parents, without even taking their clean clothes with them, the woman promising that her husband would provide them with all of the clothes they needed.

They went to Charlotte and were carried to a secluded house out in the suburbs, in a disreputable part of town. The woman refused to allow them to go on the street in the day time and kept them close, promising them that when night came that they would go out and have a good time. The little Kinley girl was dissatisfied and raised quite a disturbance. She was homesick and wanted to come back to Lexington at once. She raised such a stir that the woman thought it best, for safety, to let her come home and she sent her to the station in the care of a negro hack driver. At the station the girl was identified by officers who were seeking for her and soon both of the girls were in the hands of the officers, waiting to be carried back to their parents at Lexington. Both Mr. Kinley and Mr. Gibbs went to Charlotte at once and efforts were made there to locate the slippery couple, but to an avail. Both escaped.

From the stories of the girls it appeared that the woman and her companion intended to take them to Jacksonville, Fla. and were preparing to make their getaway when the Charlotte officers butted in. If they had managed to get out of Charlotte with their prey, it is hardly probably that the girls would have been soon recovered.

The girls are mere children. The little Gibbes girl will not be 14 until next November, although she looks to be the older of the two. The Kinley girl is just past 14 and both are unusually pretty and well-behaved. They seem very quiet, innocent children and it is not thought that they could have known anything of the horrible fate that was evidently intended for them.

After the disappearance of the couple in Charlotte nothing was heard of them for some time. The woman sent her small boy here to her mother shortly after the rescue of the girls but did not come herself. Last week she turned up here and the officers watched her every move for several days.

Saturday night Officer Welch, who did especially fine work on the case, got word that she was packing her trunks preparatory to leaving Lexington. He went to the station and found that she had purchased a ticket to Danville, Va., and had checked her trunks to that city. He "spotted" her to the conductor and came up town and called up the chief of police in Danville, Va. To him he described minutely the man and the woman and when she arrived in that city two plain clothes men were on the job. They located the man Sunday morning at about four o'clock and so notified Mr. Welch. He left on an early train for Danville and returned with his prisoner on No. 35 Sunday night. Noel did not object to coming back, though he might have stood the officer off until he could have gotten regulation papers for him. These could have been obtained with but little delay and the result would have been the same.

The case was set for two o'clock Monday before Squire J.F. Hedrick, but the defendants filed an affidavit for removal and it was turned over to Mayer Moyer, who set Monday, July 10 for that trial, at four o'clock p.m. Noels' bond was fixed at $300 and the woman was allowed to go on her own recognizance. Noel was unable to give bond and is in jail.

What Became of the Chief?

This account from the April 17, 1918 *Dispatch* could easily have had the subtitle of "Wicked Spree or No Spree":

For about two weeks now there has been much speculation in Lexington as to just what happened to Chief of Police J.H. Mingus, who is said to have left here in the morning about five o'clock, hiring a transfer owner to take him to Rowan County, his old home. Several days later a message was received here from a doctor in Winston-Salem, saying that Mr. Mingus had been brought to that place for treatment and was rather seriously sick. The fact that the police chief left here at such an unearthly hour, without even as much as notifying the authorities or sending them immediate word concerning his departure seemed rather queer to a lot of folks. The badge of the chief of police also made the trip. A former chief, who served 15 to 20 years ago, expressed his regret that the badge had disappeared so unceremoniously, saying he bought the badge when he took office and that it was still his property and he expected it to be laid away in his archives some day. Other ex-chiefs say, however, that the badge was sold to them by predecessors, but not the man who claims original ownership.

The newspaper article continues, moving from the disappearance of the chief of police and his badge to a possible late night "party" the night before Mingus's disappearance:

The sudden disappearance of Mr. Mingus and the talk it created caused certain men to investigate rumors that on the night previous to the early morning departure a "party" had been held in the chief's office on Depot Street. A great lot of bread crumbs and other remnants were found on the floor and a glass sitting in the room smelled very strong of whiskey.

The police commissions say on the contrary that they failed to find any convincing evidence that the departed chief had indulged too freely in these refreshments and quote the transfer driver as saying his passenger was entirely sober. The Winston-Salem doctor is also reported to have said there was no evidence of a spree.

In the meantime Patrolman Earnhardt has been acting chief and the police commissioners are waiting to see whether Mr. Mingus will be able satisfactorily to explain his strange absence.

The author of this book researched the outcome of this incident but could find nothing to solve the case of the missing police chief and his badge.

ASSAULT WITH ATTEMPT TO RAPE ELEVEN-YEAR-OLD GIRL

On September 11, 1947, the *Dispatch* published an article entitled, "Odell James Held To Higher Court in Assault Case: 11-Year Old Girl Is Accuser; Willie James to Marry Older Girl." The newspaper story is as follows:

Odell James, 21-year old Reedy Creek man who told investigating officers that he went through the third grade in school, was bound over to superior court at a hearing in County court here last night on a charge of assault with intent to rape upon an eleven-year old girl of this city. Bond was set at $7,500, which it was indicated James would be unable to furnish, and he will probably remain in jail until the November term.

Only the frail looking little girl took the stand for the state, and she gave her testimony in almost whispered tones as Solicitor Charles W. Mauze, Attorney for the defense and Judge Turner S. Wall gathered closely about the witness chair. None of the court room spectators heard the testimony, but the judge and attorneys agreed she had made a good witness, though once tears filled her eyes and it appeared she might break down. The distressed parents sat nearby and bent forward in anxiety.

The defendant is charged under a state statue which makes it a capital crime to have carnal knowledge of a girl under the age of twelve. He has been engaged as a furniture worker here. The child's father is with a local electrical concern.

In companion cases in which Willie James and Joe Dunn, also local furniture workers, the former a brother of Odell, charged with carnal knowledge of a girl under sixteen, were allowed bonds in the sum of $750 each and the cases continued until Monday night.

It was learned that Willie James and the girl in this case had expressed a desire to be married and the continuance was granted to permit time for this to be consummated. The procecutrix [sic] *in this case is said to be almost sixteen and appears to be fully developed. James was reported to have been going with her for several months before last Saturday night when the three young men took the girls from the home of the older about nine o'clock and did not return them until three o'clock Sunday morning, according to information gathered by investigating officers.*

Liquor Responsible for Lexington Tragedy

Sheriff Jim Leonard was shot to death on February 5, 1932. For two days, the true details of Leonard losing his life were hidden. Lexington attorney Walter Foil Brinkley and the district solicitor, George Younce, were with Leonard when he died. Wint Capel, in his book *The Good Doctor's Downfall*, explains events leading up the murder:

The three of them [Leonard, Brinkley and Younce] *had enjoyed a steak dinner at Brinkley's home in Lexington, then had motored the 20 miles to Winston-Salem, in an auto owned and driven by the sheriff, to visit with a friend of the sheriff's.*

Coming back not long before midnight, their car wrecked, or overturned. Two men in a truck stopped and went to their aid. No one was seriously hurt. The rescuers agreed to take the trio to Lexington.

En route, for some reason, a few heated words were exchanged. It would be shown later that the trio had been drinking rather heavily. Finally, the truck pulled up at Brinkley's house on Vance Circle. Brinkley and Younce made for the house, but the sheriff hung back. He kept talking to one of those with the truck, 18 year-old Nil Wimmer of Roanoke, Va. Either because Sheriff Leonard was putting some of the blame on Wimmer for the sheriff's wreck, or "for just being too damn smart," the sheriff threatened to arrest

> *him. Wimmer made it clear he didn't intend to be. Then the sheriff pulled a pistol and began firing. Wimmer fell wounded. But then so did the sheriff. He died a few hours later in the local hospital. Wimmer, with a slight abdominal wound, was placed under arrest by officers called to the scene. He was charged with murder the next day, after a coroner's inquest. The sheriff's pistol was found buried under a few inches of dirt back of the Brinkley residence. Both Younce and Brinkley had testified that Wimmer fatally wounded the sheriff.*

With that background, we'll now turn to the February 6, 1932, account in The *Dispatch.* The huge bold headlines read: YOUNCE AND BRINKLEY WILL TELL TRUTH—SHERIFF LEONARD KILLED IN STRUGGLE OVER GUN WITH SOLICITOR GEORGE YOUNCE—SOLICITOR AND ATTORNEY TO TELL CORONER'S JURY HOW IT HAPPENED—SOLICITOR HID PISTOL, LIQUOR RESPONSIBLE FOR TERRIBLE TRAGEDY. Here is the article that explains what happened next:

> *Sheriff James A. Leonard of Davidson County was accidently killed by his own pistol while Solicitor George A. Younce of the 12th judicial district struggled to wrest the gun from him after the sheriff had fired and wounded Neal Wimmer.*
>
> *Walter Foil Brinkley, Lexington lawyer and companion of Sheriff Leonard and Solicitor Younce, and the solicitor will both go before the Corner's jury as quickly as it can be reassembled and made statement to this effect.*
>
> *Mr. Brinkley and Solicitor Younce will admit that they lost their heads and attempted to conceal the sheriff's pistol and a pillow from the truck of E.R. Sullivan, which Mr. Brinkley was carrying away from the scene when the shooting began.*
>
> *Mr. Brinkley's statement this afternoon through his law partner and friend explains that the part composed of the sheriff, Solicitor and himself had been drinking.*
>
> *Horror over the awful outcome caused them to completely lose their heads, hide the pistol and pillow and to deny before the Coroner jury yesterday that they knew how the sheriff was killed.*

The February 6, 1932 issue of the *Dispatch* gives statement from both Mr. Younce and the law partner of Mr. Brinkley:

> *"Mr. Younce's Statement"*
>
> *I heard the first shot as I stood on the steps of the Brinkley porch. I dashed out to the truck and saw a fellow lying there with Jim standing*

over him. My only thought was to prevent trouble and I shouted, "Give me that gun" and grappled with the Sheriff. Two shots were fired and Jim fell. The gun was in his hand when the shots were fired. The awfulness of the situation completely unnerved me and I picked up the gun, carried it back of the garage and hid it among the weeds, saying to Brinkley as I passed, "What must I do?" Brinkley said, "Get help," and I left with that intention in mind. Brinkley went into the house.

As I was on my way up the street, I heard the ambulance and then realized that someone had already sent for assistance to the scene. Then I went on to the hotel, completely upset by the tragedy and the blow I had received in the wreck.

Unfortunately there had been drinking among us during the night.

Gold, Silver, Wood and Brass

The May 20, 1908 edition of the *Dispatch* bore a caption entitled, "Gold, Silver, Wood and Brass: Interesting Trial Over a Lot of Southern Railway Brass Which the Railway Confiscates." Here are the details:

A trial before Squire Moyer last week brought forth an array of names that reminded one of the directions for the building of the temple in Jerusalem. Two men named Wood and Siler were charged with stealing brass, and one of the lawyers bore the name of Gold. It was an interesting case, aside from the novel collection of surnames. C.L. Wood of Lexington, testified that two years ago in March or April he bought some brass from Gook Loflin, then foreman on some railroad work at the Yadkin river bridge; but who is now out of the state, so the story runs. Wood said he paid Loflin 2 cents per pound for it, and brought it to Lexington and sold it to Mr. J.L. Michael for 4 cents per pound. Mr. Michael dumped it in a box and for two years it rested in his store in plain sight of the public. He paid no attention to the matter. Not long ago a Hebrew merchant named Silver, of High Point, came along and bought the brass, 325 pounds of it, and consigned it to a firm up north, giving "Peter Cooper," as the name of the shipper. Mr. Henry L. Propst, who looks after the weighing of freight for the Southern, grew interested in the box soon as he felt its weight, and he, in the exercise of his duties, proceeded to open the box. He found Southern railway brasses. Detective Williamson rounded up Silver and Wood. Silver was discharged from the case, and Wood sent to court on his own recognizance. The brass is really worth 15 cents a pound. Messrs. Walser & Walser, S.E. Williams, W.P. Mangum Turner and Thomas J. Gold of High Point, were the lawyers in the case.

The charge in the warrant was larceny and receiving.

UNEXPECTED HOUSE GUESTS

In May 1865, Dr. William R. Holt, owner of the Homestead on North Main Street in Lexington, learned that Federal troops were approaching the town. He left his wife, Louisa, and their children in the house while he went a short distance in order to secure their Linwood plantation southwest of Lexington, where he was noted for experiments in "scientific agriculture." This is what happened next:

Union Gen. H. Judson Kilpatrick and the 9th Pennsylvania Calvary soon arrived in Lexington to patrol the county and establish order as Reconstruction began in the South. To safeguard her home from possible destruction, Mrs. Holt offered it to Kilpatrick as his headquarters. His staff officers immediately placed a United State flag at the gate and posted sentries around the house.

Although very little is recorded about the Federal army's actions while in Lexington, family traditions indicate that the house remained undamaged and that Mrs. Holt and her children were treated considerately. Even so, iron brackets remain today on the door of the girls' bedroom, evidence of Mrs. Holt's determination to safeguard them during the two months Kilpatrick's men occupied the house.

Why the iron brackets on the girls' bedroom door. Perhaps Kilpatrick's "wicked" reputation had preceded him to Lexington. Major General William T. Sherman summed up Kilpatrick's character in 1864 by saying, "I know that Kilpatrick is a hell of a damned fool, but I want just that sort of man to command my cavalry."

Hellish he was, as indicated by this historic report:

Kilpatrick continued with Sherman through his March to the Sea to Savannah and north in the Carolinas Campaign. He delighted in destroying Southern property. On two occasions his coarse personal instincts betrayed him: Confederate cavalry under the command of Maj. Gen. Wade Hampton raided his camp while he was in bed with a young Southern woman he had met while going through Columbia, and, at the Battle of Monroe's Crossroads, he was forced to flee for his life in his underclothes until his troops could reform.

Known as "Kilcavalry" (or "Kill-Cavalry") because he was notorious for his reckless disregard for human lives and "despised by southerners whose homes and towns he devastated," we can certainly understand why Louisa

Major General Judson Kilpatrick. *Courtesy of the Library of Congress.*

Wade Hampton. *Courtesy of the Library of Congress.*

Holt bolted her daughters' bedroom with iron brackets. The Holt family was lucky because when he and his troops left, "he gave the family some gold and sugar. He also gave daughter Amelia Holt a black pony that she named Kilpatrick."

Cold Blooded and Entirely Without Provocation

The front page of the October 10, 1905 *Dispatch*, presented Lexington readers with startling details following the headline "Murdered by Negro." A portion of the article is quoted here:

Early Sunday morning R.H. Eubanks, white, was killed by Oscar Gaddy, a negro, at Camp No. 1, of Lane Brothers double tracking force about two and one-half miles north of Lexington.

The crime was cold-blooded and entirely without provocation. Gaddy was in his shanty discharging his pistol. Guns are just allowed in these camps by the white foremen and whenever one is found, they take charge of it. They do this to preserve order and keep down lawlessness, and right well they succeed at it. Mr. Eubanks, who was walking boss at his camp, immediately went to the shanties and entering, asked who was doing shooting.

"I am," was the negro's reply, "and by G——, I'll shoot you."

The fatal shot followed the threat instantly. Mr. Eubanks fell and in a moment was dead. The ball entered his left side, just grazing his left arm, and passing through the heart, penetrated into the right side about the nipple, from which place it was afterward removed.

The negro, it seems was on his bunk, and was not fully dressed. He was barefooted and bareheaded, clad only in an undershirt and pants over which he wore overalls. Throwing down his gun, he ran out of the shanty and escaped.

Runners immediately came to Lexington for the officers and in a short a time as possible a posse was formed and pursuit begun. But the negro had a long lead on the pursuers and got away. He was trailed for miles across field and stream, through woods and along the roads. Every farmer in the region turned out and joined the railroad men, the officers and the citizens from town. Afoot, bareback, horseback, mule back, and in vehicles, they hunted, high and low for the murderer. A blood hound was brought down from High Point on the 2:30 train and put upon the trail. He failed to make good, whether because he was, like his kind are held to be by some, a fake, or whether the hundreds who tramped over the trail had destroyed the scent, is not clear. Some stoutly hold that the dog was not given a descent chance. Anyway, dog and men failed to catch the criminal, and the chase was given up when darkness fell.

The miserable crime aroused considerable excitement in town and those who remained at home anxiously inquired all day long for news. "Have they got him," was on everybody's lips.

Gaddy is a big negro and a bad one. He weighs about 200 pounds and is of a ginger cake shade. One of his thumbs is crooked. He is said to be from Guilford county and also from Winston. It was thought Sunday night that he was bearing toward the Southern main-line with High Point or Greensboro as an objective point.

The dead man was from Pedlar's Mills, Amherst county, Virginia. He leaves a wife and three little children. Lane Brothers had employed him here for probably six months. He was given a good name by them and by all who knew him. He had no trouble that is known with his hands and the negro who shot him is not known to have had any grudge against him. Mr. Eubanks was 38 years of age. The remains were sent to his home on No. 36 Monday morning, accompanied by the deceased's nephew, Mr. Clairborne, also of Amherst county.

CHAPTER 5

Straight from the Horse's Mouth

POOL ROOMS: "A WASTAGE OF MONEY"

The following article appeared in the April 17, 1918 issue of the *Dispatch:*

> *Pool rooms must get out of Lexington by the first of August, for no licenses will be issued after that date. The council also proposes to prevent any pool rooms being licensed within one mile of the corporate limit, if they have the*

Pool room and a group of young loafers. *Courtesy of the Library of Congress.*

legal right. Otherwise a committee from the council will appear before the board of county commissioners and press such action of them. The Council feels that now is no time to encourage the wastage of money on pool rooms when there are so many needs for every American dollar.

However, there is a "catch," as noted in the last sentence of the article: "The ordinance does not apply, of course, to those clubs where the members play pool without extra cost."

All Because She Refused a Bath

On May 8, 1930, the *Dispatch* ran a lengthy front-page story entitled, "Prisoner Uses Razor and Gun in County Jail: Two Cut When Negress Goes Wild—Pistol Fails to Fire." Just when you think you've heard it all, something like this comes to light, and this is what reportedly happened:

"Rev. C.O. Roughmays" was the only name of a negro prisoner who went berserk in the county jail here last Saturday evening, cut two other negro women prisoners with a razor and snapped a loaded pistol at two white women prisoners...But whatever her name, she was evidently rough for a few minutes at least.

Details of the incident were learned Monday evening from Dr. G.C. Gambrell, county health officer, who was called to the jail to treat the two injured women and examine the infuriated and apparently insane prisoner.

Because an effort was being made to force the preacher-prisoner who had been admitted to jail a week previous...where she is reported to have shown signs of being of unsound mind, to take a bath, she "saw red" and produced the razor from about her clothing and slashed the two women prisoners who had been directed to see that she was bathed. One of the women received a four-inch cut on the lower leg that laid the flesh open to the bone, according to Dr. Gambrell and required five stitches to close. The other was slashed to the bone across the top of the forearm. Had the cut been on the other side of the arm, death from bleeding might have happened before help could have arrived.

As if this were not wicked enough, the saga now deepens in this way:

A third negro woman prisoner, a woman of powerful stature, pushed over the razor wielder, sat upon her, twisted her arm and forced the razor to drop on the floor. Then the sitting captor ran down stairs from the upper tier of cells where negro prisoners are kept to spread the alarm, failing to pick up the razor from the floor. The door to this section was left open and the "Roughmay" woman is said to have come down to the section occupied by the white prisoners and, according to information given the health officer, snapped a loaded pistol, which she had produced from somewhere about her person, directly on two of the white women. When the woman was disarmed, it was found the pistol was loaded and the cartridges showed signs of having been snapped.

The woman refused to tell Dr. Gambrell her name, other than given above, declined to say where she was from or give any past history except to say that she was twenty-one years old and full grown. "I'm not giving out any information." She was quoted as saying though admitting she understood the questions put to her. She did relate, it was stated, that she formerly had a brother but that she could not locate him and believed that a sister she called "Queen Victoria" had made way with him.

The conclusion of the newspaper report related that the woman was taken to the state asylum for Negros at Goldsboro, and further examination indicated that the razor was not all that the Reverend C.O. Roughmays was concealing:

After Dr. Gambrell had attended to the two prisoners slashed with the razor, he had the weapon wielder examined carefully, and it was found that she had pinned to her clothing next to the body some eight or ten cloth bags containing roots and herbs, powders of some kind, some ear bobs, old teeth, and other materials sometimes regarded as "charms."

The woman is said to have worn fairly heavy clothing and a corset, making it possible to conceal the two deadly weapons that were not discovered by the officer who brought her to jail last week nor by the jail authorities until they were so threateningly produced.

Against Their Will

Davidson County Court convened in Lexington on May 7, 1930. Just before adjournment, argument began in a sensational case. There are the facts as reported in the *Dispatch* May 8, 1930:

Two young women Billie Llewellyn and Xanie Hamilton and two men Theodore Gibson and Blaine Guyer were charged with prostitution. The Llewellyn woman, who is married and not living with her husband, declared Guyer not guilty of the charge, but said he had prevented her from leaving an old house out of High Point to which she and the other young woman had been taken forcibly by Theodore Gibson. Her evidence was that Gibson badly mistreated Xanie Hamilton.

The latter swore the same against Gibson and said the occurrence was against her will. The two young women said they were taken…to the place at 9:00 at night and kept there forcibly until the next evening at 5:00 when officers broke in through a window. Both said that Gibson or Guyer, or both, had locked doors against their escape while they said they were going for food. Xanie Hamilton has married since the alleged occurrence and her husband was with her in court.

PROSTITUTION

The late 1940s local newspaper accounts present both seriously wicked court cases involving prostitution; ironically, some of the reporting is written in a rather unorthodox manner. The Thursday, August 21, 1947 issue of the *Dispatch* gave the following "prostitution" articles front-page coverage:

Street walkers. *Courtesy of the Library of Congress.*

Charlie Walser, one-armed Lexington Negro, who appealed from sentences imposed yesterday in County court on charges of prostitution with a young white woman and possessing liquor for sale, tendered guilty pleas. On the liquor charge, he was given eighteen months on the roads. On the plea to aiding and abetting in prostitution, a sentence of eight months was suspended for four years conditioned on no violation of liquor laws or laws relating to sex offenses.

The Whore's Last Shift. *Courtesy of the Library of Congress.*

The young woman is now serving an eighteen-month sentence in the women's division of the state prison. In County court Walser was given two years suspended on condition he remain out of the County, but Judge Warlick modified this portion.

The *Dispatch* of January 15, 1948, devoted the following front-page article to another case involving prostitution:

Etta Mae Hill was given four months in jail for prostitution and assignation, suspended for three years on good moral behavior, on condition she not associate with Bill Barnes and not be found within the corporate limits of Lexington. She was also taxed with costs. A ninety-day sentence against Bill Barnes on a companion charge was suspended for two years on good moral behavior, and he was fined $20 plus costs. Evidence in this case was definitely colorful.

Next is a front-page article from the April 10, 1947 issue of the *Dispatch*. The headline says, "Lexington Woman Is Banished from Salisbury Hotel," and the story follows:

A young woman booked as Rebecca Hillofield and giving Lexington as her home was fined $25 and costs and given six months in the County workhouse, to be suspended on condition she leave Rowan County at once, when convicted on a charge of prostitution.

The woman stated her husband is overseas in military service and police testified she had been living at the Milner Hotel (formerly the Ford) for about three months.

A Negro bellboy at the hotel, who it was testified, acted as procurer between the local woman and a male guest of the hotel, was sentenced to twelve months on the roads but indicated a desire to appeal the sentence.

> [She] *said she had recently had a number of teeth removed and a Salisbury dentist was doing some work for her. The Court denied her request that she be allowed to return to that city to have the work completed, saying she would have to find a dentist somewhere else.*

"White Woman, Negro Man in Alleged Orgies Here" headlined the Thursday, July 31, 1947 issue of the *Dispatch*, and this article followed:

> *Evidence indicating orgies of drinking and immorality involved white women, Negro men and white alike was produced in County court here yesterday afternoon when Clarence Walser—one-armed Negro merchant of Linwood Road, just outside the city limits and Evelyn Robbins, young white woman of the city, were found guilty of prostitution and given prison sentences.*
>
> *Walser, who made no defense to a charge of selling white liquor at his home near the small store, was given two years on the roads straight in one case and eighteen months additional in the other. The lesser sentence was suspended for five years on condition he not be found in Davidson County during that time.*
>
> *The Robbins girl was given eighteen months–2 years in the women's division of State Prison.*
>
> *Sheriff Wilfred Fritts, Deputy Foster Cook, Sergeant Ed Weisner and George Mauney, police investigation officer, conducted the raid at Walser's home. It was testified, about 2:30 Monday morning Deputy Cook said he knocked on the front door and there was no response at first but in a few minutes he observed Walser go from an unlighted room to a lighted one and attempt to dispose of the contents of a half gallon jar.*

The harlot's nurse or modern procuress. *Courtesy of the Library of Congress.*

Lodgings to let. *Courtesy of the Library of Congress.*

Evelyn Robbins, said the officer, was found asleep and apparently very drunk on the couch in the unlighted living room, with her clothing in disarray. Bed clothing in a bedroom was also disturbed and under the edge of the bed was a pair of women's shoes and a pair of step-ins. The white girl had on neither shoes nor underclothing, said the officer who also testified to other evidences of immoral conduct.

RATTLER MAKES FRONT-PAGE NEWS

The August 21, 1947 edition of the *Dispatch* ran a front-page article entitled, "Girl Finds Large Rattler on Lawn with Flashlight." No details are spared in this piece:

> *When Miss Katherine Feezor, who formerly was with the local telephone company, stepped out into the back yard of her home near High Rock a few nights ago and turned the beam from a flashlight on a snake just a step away, she did what the average person would do. She jumped high and yelled. But if she had realized it was a timber rattler, she would probably have jumped a little higher and yelled a bit louder.*
>
> *As it was, Miss Feezor's father, A.W. Feezor, well known farmer, and brother Paul, hurried out and observed that the object was a rattler, lying quietly with head raised a few inches, as if in bewilderment. Paul secured a shotgun and shot off the snake's head. It proved to be about four feet long, was about three inches at its largest diameter and bore eight rattles. These did not begin buzzing until after the snake's head had departed. The big snake was only about ten feet from the back doorstep. Miss Feezor's trepidation was not lessened by the fact that she was barefooted at the time she espied the snake near her on the closely cropped grass.*
>
> *Mr. Feezor said this was the first rattler he could recall being killed on his place. However, one reported having thirteen rattles was said to have recently been killed about a mile down the Yadkin from there.*

MOONSHINE

According to the February 28, 1947 edition of the *Dispatch*, William Melton "talked himself squarely into the Davidson County jail. The newspaper printed the sage of Melton's adventure:

> *Melton also brought about the arrest of his brother-in-law, Coy McKenzie and the seizure of a small mountain moonshine still and a gallon and a half of fresh moonshine liquor.*
>
> *Melton is said to have gone to the home of Deputy Shoaf, who was in nursing a cold, Saturday afternoon about 4:00 and reported that he had been "double crossed" and wanted to "spill some beans."*

Illicit distillation of liquors: the southern mode of making whiskey. *Courtesy of the Library of Congress.*

> *He confided, said the officer, that the brother-in-law, Coy McKenzie was operating a still and accompanied him to the place of operation, about a mile and a half west of Tyro School. Sure enough, there was an all-copper distilling outfit neatly fashioned, with a still capacity of about 35 gallons, said the officer.*
>
> *But the trouble started for Melton McKenzie, according to the officer, when headmitted his interest in the distillery but declared Melton was an equal partner. Other members of the family were said to have corroborated McKenzie. Melton was drinking, said Officer Shoaf, and was reported to have told neighbors he wanted to get in jail." He did.*

Wild Drive through Lexington

Printed in the September 5, 1932 issue of the *Dispatch*, in one of those "I can't believe that really happened" true episodes, this article reported a wild drive:

A.B. Aires, young Statesville man and his mother, Mrs. T. Aires, face a group of charges in recorder's court here tonight as a result of a wild drive through Lexington about 5:30 yesterday afternoon and an encounter with I.E. Hunt, State Highway patrolman, who overhauled them.

Aires is charged with drinking under the influence of an intoxicant and with resisting arrest, Mrs. Aires faces charges of reckless driving and interferences with an officer.

The patrolman is said to have overhauled the car about two miles northeast of the city on Highway 10 when it had forced other vehicles to the shoulders of the road or into the ditch. Aires was placed under arrest and a young woman in the car, reported to have been his sister, took the wheel for the trip to the police station. En route, it is alleged, Mrs. Aires exchanged to the driver seat, turned off Main and sped down State Street, declining to stop at the municipal building. The dash continued down State to Eighth Avenue and on through the southwest section of the city until the car was blocked near Wabena [sic] *Mill.*

The two charged are reputed to have been recalcitrant about getting out of the car and when the officer placed the woman under arrest, the son is alleged to have attacked him and pushed him backward across his motorcycle. Several other men, called by the officer during the chase, arrived about this time. The officer is reported to have used a billy on Aires, who is alleged to have kicked him twice. Aires is also alleged to have made an attempt to strike D.S. Siceloff, city commissioner, with handcuffs that had been placed about his wrists by citizens who were assisting the officer and Mr. Siceloff retaliated with a blow from his cane. One of the women then struck him with a rock.

A small flask of home brew was found in the car, but no charge was placed in connection with this.

It was considerably remarkable that no accident occurred the wild dash of a mile or more through the city, with several sharp turns made at high speed.

STATUTORY RAPE

The August 26, 1948 issue of the *Dispatch* ran an article entitled, "Enoch Truitt Is Accused of Rape: Girls Ten and Eleven Are Alleged Victims." Here are the details:

> *Enoch Truitt, Negro formerly residing here, but who reportedly left Lexington by automobile last Friday morning, was arrested by Durham police yesterday and held for Lexington police on two charges of statutory rape. Officers were dispatched to Durham this morning by Chief W.R. Lanning to bring Truitt here for hearing. He is being held without bond.*
>
> *Two Negro girls whose ages were reported to police at ten and eleven charged that Truitt had abused them sexually. State statute makes carnal knowledge of a girl under twelve rape, which is punishable by death.*
>
> *Truitt had presumably left here for Snow Hill, Md., in a 1938 model Buick car, and the charges were preferred several hours later. A police radio alarm was sent out for him and officers were watching in several states.*

Remembrances of Segregated Lexington

In his book *Three Weeks in October*, Lexington, North Carolina native Charles A. Moose relates his experiences growing up in a segregated area:

> *I was born into a middle-class family in August 1953. I don't know how old I was when I first began to understand the difference between black people and white people, but it was pretty early. I understood that all the black kids went to one school, and all the white kids went to another school. And I understood that other things were separated, too. I don't remember anyone explaining this to me. It was just a fact. Explaining it would have been like explaining gravity.*
>
> *There was one movie theater in Lexington, and it had two entrances. There was the main entrance, under the marquee, where the box office was. That was for white people. They'd go in, stand in line for the popcorn and candy, and sit down where they sat.*
>
> *All the restaurants in town were the same way. We used to get barbecue from a place in town called City Barbecue. There were two rooms. One was where white people sat down and ate or ordered their food to take out. The other was for the black people.*
>
> *My parents made sure I understood things like that. They didn't tell me* why *this was the way it was. But they made sure I understood it was important. You used this door, not that door. You drank from this drinking fountain, not that drinking fountain.*

In addition to different rules for Lexington citizens, a threat of violence sometimes followed if his brother and sister and friends disobeyed those rules. This is what could happen:

> *A few blocks over from Smith Avenue was a juke joint called the Do Drop Inn. That was a sort of boundary. You didn't go past that corner, especially after dark, unless you were interested in real trouble. There was a market on another corner, around where Oak Street or Hickory Street came in, and sometimes we'd be sent down there after school or in the evening to pick something up. You understood that was another boundary. You didn't go past there, especially at night, or else you were running the risk of getting hurt.*
>
> *Or worse than hurt. The Ku Klux Klan was very active in our town. They marched down Main Street. They held rallies on the outskirts of town. They burned crosses in the fields. Once, in the town where my father's mother lived, they burned a cross on a man's front lawn.*
>
> *My father, for that reason, always carried a gun. He wore it when he went out. He kept it in his car. It was a little "Saturday night special"*

Jitterbugging in a juke joint on Saturday. *Courtesy of the Library of Congress.*

Drummer in a juke joint. *Courtesy of the Library of Congress.*

pistol. He didn't have a license for it, and he didn't advertise it. But he didn't go out without it, either. He wore it for protection. A lot of men did. You'd hear them talking about something that had happened. You'd hear them talking about using their guns.

Everybody was afraid of the Klan. Everybody was afraid that one day they'd come. Nobody knew what was going to happen. The newspaper was always full of stories about crimes that black people had supposedly committed against white people. There was always a story about a black man raping a black woman. Remember, this was not that far away from the time of "eyeball rape," when a black man could be beaten or even lynched for "eyeballing" a white woman—just for looking at her. When I was in high school, I knew a couple of boys who were always sneaking around with these white girls who were interested in black boys. There was a lot of talk about what would happen to them if anyone found out. The assumption was they would be killed.

It took a trip to the circus in Greensboro for Charles Moose and his family to realize that segregated cafes were not restricted to Lexington:

Segregated hamburger stand. *Courtesy of the Library of Congress.*

> *I remember when I was five or six years old, we had gone to Greensboro, about forty miles from Lexington, to see the circus. My mother and father had scraped and saved their money to take us, me and my brother and sister, to the big circus in the big city. And it was wonderful. We had a great day. We stopped in at this hamburger place. My dad said, "Go on, now. You go on up to the counter and tell the man what you want."*
>
> *We stood at the counter, my dad and me. I was all excited, ready to place our order, and the kid behind the counter said, "What are you doing here? We don't serve niggers here."*
>
> *We went back to the car and drove away. We didn't stop to eat anywhere else. My father was quiet all the way home. It was very traumatizing for him to have us see that happen to him and his family. I had never seen anyone hurt my dad, until that moment.*

Wicked days of Moose's childhood eventually turned to days of glory when he, as a police chief, led in Washington, D.C., one of the most suspenseful manhunts in our nation's history.

CHAPTER 6

And the Beat Goes On

SHOPLIFTING

The February 16, 1952 issue of the *Dispatch* ran the following article entitled, "Sentence Suspended On Shoplifting Charge":

> *Sarah Garris, a 20-year-old resident of South Main Street was given a four-month sentence, suspended for one year, in Davidson County Court this morning by acting Judge Ross Craver, after pleading guilty to shoplifting a baby's dress from W.T. Grant Co.*
>
> *The value of the dress was less than $2. Mrs. Garris stated that she could not afford to buy clothes for her baby, so she was forced to take the dress. She said that she had never done anything of this nature before but that she was not receiving enough money from her husband, from whom she is separated, to support her family.*
>
> *An employee of Grant's testified that Mrs. Garris denied taking the dress until she was searched and it was found beneath her clothing.*

"Man Is Alleged Leader of Shoplifting Youths" was the title of a February 7, 1956 article in the local newspaper and was reported in this manner:

> *A 29-year old resident of the Pugtown section near Lexington has been arrested on four counts of larceny and receiving and is allegedly the leader of a gang of youths who have admitted a series of shoplifting raids in*

A boy beside a store window display of Christmas ornaments. *Courtesy of the Library of Congress.*

Lexington, Thomasville and other cities. The man is Sterling Berry, whose address is C.C. 12, Lexington.

Berry, according to officers, took the youths to Thomasville and was with them when they stole two electric razors and one portable radio. He was also with one of the boys who stole a portable radio from Robertson's Radio shop in Lexington. Berry, according to the lawmen, had sold a portable radio and one of the electric razors in Lexington.

Jerry Joe "Buddy" Ellis, 10, who lives on Hemstead Street has admitted to stealing the following items: an airplane motor from Lanier Hardware, a model plane, two bottles of paint and two tubes of glue from the Hobby Shop, a model car from Grants, a box of shotgun shells and a box of .22 cartridges from Corley Home and Auto Supply Company, flashlight batteries from Community Drug Store; cigarettes from Everhart's Gulf Service Station; a portable radio from Robertson's Radio Shop, and five boxes of .22 cartridges from the Firestone place at Salisbury.

Jimmy Lyons, 16, of R. 8, admitted taking an airplane motor from Lanier Hardware; a portable radio and a pellet gun from Sears in Winston-Salem, and a portable radio from a Thomasville shop.

By 1960, shoplifting had become a major concern in Lexington. An Anti-Shoplifting Clinic, sponsored by the Lexington Merchants Association, was held at the Carolina Theatre. This clinic was announced in the November 7, 1960 issue of the local newspaper and gave the following information:

An interesting and helpful anti-shoplifting clinic will be held here next Tuesday morning…All merchants and employees in local stores are invited to attend, at no charge…Stores will delay their opening hour on Tuesday morning until 9:30, so that personnel can attend the clinic.

Paul D. Schiller, a former FBI agent, will conduct the clinic. He is now head of Paul D. Schiller and Associates of Raleigh, and has conducted similar clinics which were very successful in a number of other cities.

Schiller will explain methods for detecting shoplifters, as well as actions which can be taken to prevent or curtail this despicable practice. He will give demonstrations and show photographs to illustrate his points.

Arrangements for the clinic were made by Ardell Lanier, director of the local Merchants Association and also a director in the North Carolina Merchants Association. The local association is paying for the clinic, with no charge for attendance.

Shoplifting is quite prevalent here, probably costing merchants considerably more than many of them realize. Police get frequent complaints, and although some of the offenders are caught, many others go undetected.

Apparently, the clinic produced successful results, as there were fewer newspaper reports of shoplifting after this date.

Obscene Mail

The May 20, 1959 issue of the *Dispatch* printed an article entitled, "Obscene Mail Menace Growing." And its contents were aimed at protecting the youth of Lexington, as reported:

A million American boys and girls of high school and junior high school age may receive obscene literature and pictures in the mail this year, even though they neither wanted or solicited it, Postmaster Roby Maley said today.

The Postal Inspection Service, he stated, on the basis of available facts has estimated that dealers in smut are sending such materials to children at a rate of 700,000 to 1,000,000 mailings a year.

"It is quite possible that children here in Lexington are unwittingly being carried on lists used by mail order pornographer houses to solicit sales of their filthy materials, Maley said.

The local Post Office has joined in an intensive campaign launched nationally by Postmaster General Arthur E. Summerfield to stamp out what the Postmaster General has described as "a vile racket of huge proportions."

Mailman. *Courtesy of the Library of Congress.*

Using first class postage which protects the mail from inspection, filth peddlers send out lewd circulars by the hundreds of thousands, solicit orders from youngsters for obscene movies, photographs, comic books, slides, and similar material.

"It is shocking to realize," Maley said, "that sales of such trash amount to half a billion dollars a year, the Post Office estimates."

In a recent speech, he noted, Postmaster General Summerfield stated that police records and sociological studies show that a link exists between addiction to pornography and the increasing rate of sex crime.

The Post Office in recent years urged legislation which would permit prosecution not only at the point of mailing of obscene material, but in the communities where it is received.

Such legislation was passed by the 85th Congress and signed by President Eisenhower last year.

The Post Office Department, Maley said, is determined to use this new legal weapon to the fullest possible extent. It has already assisted in apprehending and prosecuting dealers in obscenity such as a couple—a man and his wife—who recently received a ten-year prison sentence in Boise, Idaho, following mailings made from California and Oregon.

To make full use of the new law, however, the Post Office makes it clear that it needs the corporation of parents and decent-minded citizens throughout the nation. To help achieve this cooperation, the Postmaster General and postmasters in every part of the country have launched a special program for nationwide action. They believe that, if this program is successful, the victimizing of children by dealers in filth can be stamped out.

Driver Is Charged with Embezzlement

The smaller headline read, "Leroy Best Under Bond: Probation Probable In Cloth Theft At Mill." The following is the complete article, as printed in the December 17, 1945 issue of the *Dispatch*:

> *Leroy Best, employed for some time as truck driver for Coble's in the sales division, had been arrested by local police and placed under a $100 bond for hearing in County court on a charge of embezzlement. It is alleged in the warrant that Best appropriated to his own use some ten gross of Eskimo pies and quantities of ice cream in quart packages and Dixie cups. The total value of the merchandise charged against the accused in the warrant is placed at $206.*
>
> *It was indicated the dairy concern would seek to prove that Best had from time to time sold quantities of products placed in his charge and had kept the proceeds for himself. The warrant is returnable in County court Friday.*

Eskimo Pie truck. *Courtesy of the Library of Congress.*

A movie star eating an Eskimo Pie.
Courtesy of the Library of Congress.

Recently another truck driver for the same concern was tried for embezzlement of a quantity of whole milk and placed under suspended sentence.

At Friday's session of the court, Samuel Hailey pled guilty to the larceny of a roll of cloth, said to contain about sixty yards, from the Dacotah cotton mills. The cloth is said to have been recovered from him by the police. Judge Turner Wall continued prayer for judgment until next Wednesday, and in the meantime the case is being studied by T.D. Stokes, district probation officer. Hailey is married and has three children, it is reported. Police said he had no previous court record.

TAXI DRIVER ARRESTED FOR EMBEZZLEMENT OF $9.20

My research did not produce many reported cases of embezzlement, so that must not have been one of the more wicked actions in early Lexington—or perhaps it just was not reported. The September 29, 1949 edition of the *Dispatch* did run the following piece:

> *Avery L. Eason, 29, local taxicab driver, was in Davidson county jail here this morning on a charge of embezzlement after his arrest by police officers last night.*
>
> *Eason was taken into custody by officers at his home on East Third Avenue. He was charged with the alleged taking of fares collected during a part day's work with Red Bird Taxi company of this city.*
>
> *Officers said they received a report from officials of the cab concern Monday and had been on the search for Eason since that time. It is believed he had been out of town a short while and then returned to his home here.*
>
> *An official of the local cab concern said today Eason had driven part of his shift Monday and had taken off for his evening meal. He stated the man had not returned to work after the meal. A check with company files showed $9.10 missing, the spokesman stated.*

The official said he received a report later Monday that Eason was seen trying to thumb a ride in the direction of Salisbury. A report was then made to the police.

Mashed Yellow Apple in Bank Robbery Bag

Before four bandits robbed the Denton Bank, on September 5, 1932, they stopped by a store in the Black Ankle section of Montgomery County Tuesday morning and purchased four yellow apples. They had a strangc request of the merchant:

They requested that the apples be placed in a large paper bag, one corresponding to the bag in which the money was placed at the bank. A mashed yellow apple was found in the abandoned car, Deputy Bowers said yesterday, so it appeared evident that the approach to Denton was made by a circuitous route from the south. The report that five men were in the car that stopped on the road beyond the covered bridge near Flint Hill gave ground for belief that a companion of the robbers was awaiting with another car near the covered bridge. The woman who reported seeing the car stop momentarily and then speed away could not tell the officers the make of the car except that it was a coach or sedan.

Earlier, three men had entered the bank, and this scene played out, according to the *Dispatch* article on September 5, 1932:

Three men entered the bank while Chisholn Disher, Denton oil dealer, was at the teller's cage preparing to make a deposit. The smaller of the two, a young man estimated to weigh only about 125 pounds, made his way around behind the cage to the vault. The larger of the trio came up in front of the cage to the vault. The larger of the two came up in front of the cage, while the third stood nearer the door, which is on one side of the building front.

"Huddy, give me that," said one of the robbers, reaching over the counter and possessing Mr. Bisher's cash, about $200. Thinking someone was "kidding" him, Mr. Disher is quoted as saying he reached for his money, but instead looked into the end of a pistol barrel. His hands went up, while the other man in front of the cage covered Baxter Carter, acting cashier. While Mr. Carter was forced to hold open a large paper bag, the man inside scooped up the cash and dumped it in, taking about $5,500 in addition to that secured from Mr. Disher.

WICKED POLIO STRIKES LEXINGTON

The summer of 1948 saw a polio epidemic in North Carolina, and Lexington did not escape the dreaded disease.

By July 22, newspaper headlines proclaimed the bad news: "Thirteen Polio Cases Set Record for This County." The health officer gave comparative figures:

> *Two more cases of polio in Davidson County which had been confirmed yesterday by the County health department brought the 1948 total to thirteen, counting one local child that became ill a few days after out of the County on a vacation, said Dr. G.C. Gambrell, County health officer.*
>
> *The figure as compared to those of 1947 are not in themselves alarming, said Dr. Gambrell, though he added that the prospect is not cheering. Last year Davidson County had eleven cases of the disease reported to the department. But, the first of these occurred in August and the others were reported at intervals until in November, the health officer records show. Five of last year's cases occurred in the Denton section, where so far this year there has been no outbreak.*
>
> *At this date last year, there was not a reported case of polio in Davidson County.*
>
> *1944 is looked upon as the year of the great polio epidemic in North Carolina, when the largest number of reported cases occurred in any year on record. Present figures for the State are already well ahead of that year. Davidson County had only ten cases that year, said the health officer.*
>
> *In 1943 no cases were reported; there were four in 1945 and three in 1946.*

A flier for the President's Birthday Ball, held to fight infantile paralysis. *Courtesy of the Library of Congress.*

By July 25, 1948, children were not permitted to attend Sunday school during the polio epidemic. Swimming pools were closed, and children were restricted to their yards.

The August 16, 1948 front-page article elaborated with headlines that stated, "Two More Cases Polio Reported Since Thursday":

"Mrs. J.L. Cathell, Wife of Local Physician, Is Among Victims"

According to the County Health department this morning no new cases of infantile paralysis had been reported since Saturday, and one suspected case at the hospital had been diagnosed as…Meningitis, that of Leo Roberts sixteen years old, of Lexington, Rt. 3. He became ill last Wednesday.

The count of polio cases had reached a total of 41 on Saturday with two additional persons in the city limits of Lexington ill. Mrs. Drusilla Martin Cathell, wife of Dr. J.L. Cathell was taken to Lexington Memorial hospital Thursday afternoon and a spinal test showed that she is suffering from polio, though her case is described as mild. She has suffered no paralysis thus far and is improving rapidly.

Mrs. Cathell had been suffering with what was apparently a bad cold or summer flu for several days before she was taken to the hospital. Her husband has also been a hospital patient with flu. Dr. Cathell is acting County health officer. Mrs. Cathell is one of the most popular young matrons of the city and is active in civic and social circles.

According to the same article, adults were not the only ones struck by this contagious disease:

On Friday afternoon little Charles Brummett, seven-year-old son of Mr. and Mrs. Carl B. Brummett, of 426 West Sixth avenue was diagnosed as a polio patient by Dr. Dermot Lohr at Lexington Memorial hospital. He was entered in Greensboro polio center the same day for treatment. He became ill on Wednesday.

The Winston-Salem Journal reported on Saturday that John F. Metters, 14, of this county, who has been under treatment in the polio division at Baptist hospital had been sent on Friday to the convalescent center at Camp Sutton.

Little Miss Martha Ellen Miller, nine-year-old daughter of Mr. and Mrs. Vann Miller, was taken from Winston-Salem to Camp Sutton last Tuesday, for convalescence. Mr. and Mrs. Miller visited her yesterday and were informed that her recovery might be a long process. She still has weakness in her right leg. Martha Ellen is in a ward with about twenty little girls near her age, now that she is no longer quarantined, and appears happy. The Millers were favorably impressed with the splendid facilities at the convalescent center where two doctors from the National Foundation are members of the staff. Children at convalescent centers are allowed to receive mail and gifts, but those in isolation centers may not.

1903 WAS A VERY WICKED YEAR IN LEXINGTON

August 5, 1903: *A large party of revenue officers made another raid in Boon township Monday afternoon. This is the second or third raid within the past week or two. They found two barrels of liquor, arrested L.L. Davis and seized his team and wagon. Mr. Davis promptly gave a $1000 bond and was released from custody.*

The nine barrels of liquor captured by revenue officers...was carried to Salisbury and placed in the rectifying establishment of Clark Bros. for safe keeping. This liquor was stolen, presumably by the original owners, last Friday night or between three and four o'clock Saturday morning. The rectifying house adjoins Ludwick & Black's stables. And entrance was gained through the cellar door at the rear of the building, opening on an alley-way, the door, which is a double one, being forced in the middle to a sufficient extent to allow a saw to be used upon the wooden bars. Two wagons must have been used to carry off the nine barrels. The liquor is said to have been worth over $500.

Revenue officers began a search for the stolen liquor immediately after its loss was discovered. They came over to Boon township, where the liquor and the still producing it were originally seized. It is thought the officers received some information as to the whereabouts of the stolen liquor. Five of these barrels were found at one place in this County yesterday. Two of the five barrels were nearly empty, one of these containing only one gallon and the other about nine gallons of liquor.

Composite of five moonshining scenes. *Courtesy of the Library of Congress.*

The body of a white man was seen floating down the Yadkin river, near N.A. Pebble's ferry, early yesterday morning. Mr. J.D. Burton was the first to discover the body and he got in a boat and towed out in the river and towed his gruesome find to the shore... Tying the body to a stake, he immediately notified the proper officers of his find and an inquest was held… The man's shirt was saturated with blood and all the circumstances point to murder. The verdict of the coroner's jury was that his death was caused by a blow on the back of the head. A gash about three inches long was found on his head, and it is presumed he was killed and then thrown in the river.

The dead man is of medium size, weighs about 135 pounds, and looks to be 25 or 30 years of age. He was fairly well dressed, smoothly shaved and wore a heavy gold band ring on his hand. The only evidence of identification on his body was a receipt for $1.50 to E.H. Bruce from J.T. Parnell. Parnell lives at Mocksville and this receipt may throw some light on the identification of the man found in the river.

August 12, 1903: *Sheriff Dorsett received a phone message Monday evening saying that Alice Hoover, a negro woman, had died at Yadkin College and that there was strong suspicion that her death was the result of a brutal beating received at the hands of her husband, Dave Hoover. A warrant for the latter was asked for. Sheriff Dorsett immediately communicated with County Coroner C. A. Julian and these officers went out to Yadkin College early yesterday morning. An inquest was deemed necessary and Coroner Julian summoned for this purpose Messrs. Ed. L. Greene, Daniel Phillips, Alvaron Leonard, J.T. Williamson, M.F. Phillipps and W.T. Totten. These gentlemen, after hearing much testimony and witnessing an autopsy performed on this woman by the coroner, rendered a verdict that "deceased came to her death from unknown causes."*

On Saturday, July 25th, Dave Hoover, husband of the dead woman, gave her an unmerciful beating. Hoover ran away immediately. Since the beating the woman has constantly complained of pains in her side. Her rather sudden death on Monday naturally led the public to attribute the cause to the beating she had received. However, the coroner and his jury after a careful examination and autopsy found no bruises or marks of violence whatever on her person. There was sufficient evidence before the jury as to the whipping of the woman but nothing whatever to indicate that his whipping caused her death.

Dave Hoover has been away since whipping his wife, but came home early yesterday morning. He evidently anticipated some unpleasant revelations and left in a few hours. Diligent search was made for him by the Sheriff and his officers yesterday, but he could not be found.

Last Saturday night at Haden's Grove at a negro "festible," [sic] *in the famous Boone township of Davidson County, one negro shot and killed another. Walter Simmons is the one that did the shooting, and Ernest Smith the one killed. They were brothers-in-law. No previous trouble between them is known. Simmons went to the festival and said he was looking for trouble, wanted to get him a man. Simmons, talking to Smith said you don't believe powder will burn, do you? Smith said no. You don't believe I'll shoot you? And again Smith said no, thereupon Simmons shot Smith between the eyes and killed him. Simmons tried to escape but was captured Sunday morning by Hoke Harrison and Horace Simmerson and the preliminary hearing was had same day before Justices H.C. Grubb, Frank Snider and W.D. Simmerson and the murderer was committed to jail without bail, and he is now safely lodged in a steel cell at this place.*

He will be tried at August term of court which begins on the 24th instant, when it is to be hoped he will get justice..

It has been a long time since anyone was convicted of murder in Davidson [County] *but from all reports the jury will have to return a verdict of guilty. Sheriff Dorsett will evidently have an unpleasant duty to perform during his present term of office.*

The Dispatch *man called at the jail Monday to interview Simmons. The negro is 25 years old, has been working at High Point for Mr. Jesse Hayden and had gone home to see his family. He says he killed Smith, but did not intend to do it, that they were playing, that neither one was mad, that Smith had a shovel drawn over him and had hold of the barrel of the pistol when he fired. Simmons says he stayed at home that night, but could not sleep good, that on Sunday morning he went to see Esquire Frank Snider who advised him to surrender and that he was on his way to Esquire R.B. Thompson's to give himself up when the officers arrested him. Simmons is not a bad looking negro and seems to be fairly intelligent. He don't appear to be worried about his case. The* Dispatch *man told him he was in a bad fix and would probably hang and change countries [sic], and Simmons replied, yes I expect so.*

Corn liquor was flowing fairly freely and Simmons says Smith was drinking but that he was sober.

The following passages were found in the court's criminal docket for Saturday, September 2, 1903:

J.J. Biesecker, retailing: pled guilty. Sentenced to six months in jail.

Walter Simmons, col. Pled guilty to murder in second degree of Ernest Smith, col. Judgment: 15 years in penitentiary.

Fred Hargrave, col. Was found guilty of slandering a Mrs. J.P. Vuncanon, a white woman. He was sentenced to 10 months hard labor on Lexington township roads.

Horace Adams, the negro found guilty of an assault with deadly weapon on his father, was ordered to work with the chain gang on our township roads for six months.

Henry Leonard and wife were found guilty of retailing liquor. This was their first offense, and his Honor continued judgment on payments of costs and ordered defendants to give a $100 bond to appear from court to court and show they have not again transgressed the law.

Ed. And Henderson Imbler were tried under a charge of nuisance. They were found guilty and each fined $5 and cost. Their attorney gave notice of an appeal to the Supreme court.

The burglary case against Pleas. Oakes was changed to larceny or to receiving stolen goods. He was convicted of the latter charge and sentenced to work on the roads for nine months.

Burrell Hollard, the lad who attempted to burn up a brick block [sic] *in Lexington some time ago in order to wreak vengeance upon his employer, was found guilty of two attempts to set fire to store houses. On account of his youth his sentence was light—12 months on the roads.*

Jake Everhart pled guilty to breaking in Peacock & Adderton's store and was tried and found guilty of breaking open Rothrock, Weaver & Co's. shops. He was sentenced to seven years at hard labor in the penitentiary.

A.L. Satterwhite, an insurance agent, who has been operating in Lexington and Davidson county for the past year, was convicted of obtaining money under false pretense and was sentenced to 12 months on the public roads of Lexington township. The defendant appeals to the Supreme court. His bond was fixed at $500. This he gave and was released from custody pending the appeal.

D.H. Koonts, who was arraigned upon the charge of digging up a tobacco plant bed of J.E. Miller was found not guilty.

John May pled guilty to the charge of false pretense and judgment was suspended on payment of costs.

The jury returned a verdict of not guilty as to Curt Thomas, colored, charged with perjury.

Tobacco flower. *Courtesy of the Library of Congress.*

A true bill was found against A. Evans, who is alleged to have been conducting a government distillery in the Boon township in open defiance of the Watts law. A warrant against Evans was issued, but he couldn't be found.

And lest we not forget the antics of Baxter Shemwell, he was also on the Davidson County Court docket for that busy day of September 1, 1903. This is what Mr. Shemwell was up to at this time:

A true bill was also returned against Baxter Shemwell for carrying concealed weapons, and for drawing a pistol on Mr. Z.I. Walser. A capias [sic] *was issued and sent to the Sheriff of Buncombe county, with instruction to arrest Shemwell and have him placed under a $200 justifiable bond for his appearance for trial at the February term of Davidson Superior Court.*

MOB LYNCHES THREE

From various newspaper reports, it seems that August 1905 produced some horrendous events. The following are true *Dispatch* articles:

"MOB LYCHES THREE: Negroes Accused of Killing Lyerly"

Monday night about 11 o'clock a mob of about 23,000 men took three of the accused Lyerly murders from the Rowan jail and hung them on the outskirts of Salisbury. The three negroes lynched were Nease and John Gillesple and Jack Dillingham. George Ervin was questioned by the mob, and then returned to his cell in the jail. The women prisoners were also spared.

The mob began to gather about nine o'clock. Judge Long had opened the special court for the trial of the negroes, and the grand-jury had found true bills.

Vague reports had come to the court that lynching was talked of, and Judge Long turned his attention to lawlessness. He charged the jury to regard to lynching and late Monday afternoon called in the grand jury and read them the law. He spoke hopefully that the people would not attempt a lynching. Even while he was talking, the trouble was forming.

From nine to eleven o'clock the streets about the jail swarmed with people. Solicitor Hammer, Senator Overman, Judge Long, and other well-known men addressed the mob and urged the people to desist, all to no purpose. The military company was ordered out, and came with guns loaded with blank cartridges. They angered the crowd all the more and when the determination to lynch the negroes was finally ripe, the military company with its guns doubled quickly up the street. It had no orders to shoot to kill. Special armed deputies were also on the scene, but were useless. The three accused negroes were taken from their cells and carried to the vicinity of the baseball ground…and there were strung up. The bodies were riddled with bullets and death came quickly.

Before killing them, they were given a chance to confess. Nease and Jack refused either to deny or confess, but John protested his innocence with tears in his eyes.

At midnight all was over. The other prisoners were hurried out of town on a late train. These were Henry Lee, George Ervin and Bella Dillingham.

We understand that the lynching took place at the identical spot where Harris and James Gillespie, sons of Neuse Gillespie, were lynched June 11th, 1902, for the murder of Miss Cornelia Benson on June 9th, 1902. A mob of three hundred took them from jail and lynched them at 2 o'clock in the morning. Pictures were taken of the two Gillespie boys as they hung from the tree and several were gotten out of Lexington yesterday when it was realized the father of the two boys was lynched where his sons were put to death.

The tone and mood and voice of the June 14, 1909 article gets even more specific in this April 14, 1909 *Dispatch* article entitled, "The Story of a Lynching," presented here in its entirety:

"How Two Davidson County Lads Dealt With a Little Niger Boy Many Years Ago"

The other day while two Dispatch men were waiting for a train at the Salisbury Junction, Mr. Ed Hennessee, who presides over the fodder department in the union station, came up and passed and repassed [sic] *the time o' day. Presently up came Captain Ernest Koontz, a Davidson county man, who is one of the best conductors on the Southern railway. It was his train The* Dispatch *men were waiting on, some being bound for Asheville.*

"Did Koontz ever tell you about that lynching?" asked Mr. Hennessee.

"Now look here men," expostulated Conductor Koontz, "I have always been your friend, but if you publish anything this fellow says about any lynching, I will be your friend no more. It would be awful to sever such a close, life-long relationship for nothing," and the railroad man almost wept.

"Tell us about it, then," demanded the newspaper men "or what Hennessee says goes," this with a wave or pencil and pad.

And being thus forced, when his train started, and he had a breathing spell between stations, Conductor Koontz related how he and his brother Eugene, of Lexington, in the long ago negotiated a near lynching that, as recounted by the conductor, was the funniest thing you ever heard.

"But don't publish it, for the Lord's sake," pleaded the man in blue clothes and brass buttons. "You'll get me in jail sure!"

The promise not to publish was promptly given and following is the story:

Mrs. Mary Green, grandmother of Ernest and Eugene, living out in Tyro township, could not bring herself to leave the old homeplace after all her children had grown up, married and founded homes of their own, so she stayed. The children argued with her to live with them without avail, and finally a little nigger boy was secured to stay at the house and help around. Mrs. Green thought a lot of the lad, and treated him well. His name was Billie.

Meantime the negro Alf Long had killed old man Jack McBride and his wife in Tyro township, which crime occurred some 26 years ago, and had been caught and lynched. The Koontz boys were too young to have anything to do with the lynching, of course, but as boys will do, they thought a good deal about the lynching and for all the writer knows may have been hanging around when the hanging occurred. Anyway when the little nigger boy some time later ran away from their grandmother's, thereby causing the old lady much distress, the youngsters were naturally indignant and sore on the dusky lad. Conductor Koontz said that when grandmother sent word that the boy had run away, the relatives gathered and got hoes and picks cant [sic] *hooks, scythes and rakes and spades and shovels and fish poles, and so on, and turned in search of the run-away, finding him after diligent search somewhere near, or may be* [sic] *inside of, Devil's Den, or Boone's Cave, out on the Yadkin.*

One day after this Eugene and Ernest were sent to the old home place with a bunch of cattle and sheep to put in the big, unoccupied pastures. They took along some salt for the stock. Having driven the cattle into the pasture, they sat down to rest, when who should come up but the little nigger boy, a-riding of a steer that their grandmother had given him for his own special use. He had a rope bridle on the steer and was riding and grinning in characteristic fashion, which unsettled the Koontz boys muchly.

Captain Koontz says it was Eugene and Eugene says it was the conductor, but anyways, one of them suggested that the negro boy should be lynched in the fashion that the Mc____ murderer was hanged, for worrying their grandmother so much by running away. No sooner said than done, and away went the two after the negro, telling him they were going to hang him. His neck was fastened to one end of the rope and the other end of it was thrown over a limb, Billie being told solemnly in the meanwhile that he could pray if he wanted to. Seeing blood in their eyes, the little ape began to pray fervently, and almost killed his soon-to-be-murderers by praying for them and asking the Lord not to do anything with them for killing him. Having finished, Ernest kicked the steer in the ribs and he shot out from under the tree, leaving the negro swinging by the neck. Instantly the two white boys saw what they were doing and Ernest abounded up the scrubby pine tree like lightening to cut the rope. Before they got the boy down, he was almost dead. They turned doctors then, all their venge-ance [sic] *coming out, and worked heroically to resuscitate the young African. This they did, but there was a raw, red ring around his neck which looked mighty funny. They promised him they would let him go if he would promise not to tell, and if grandmother asked what the ring of red amid the black could mean, he was to say that in riding his steer, he passed swiftly under a limb and it took him a swipe on the neck. The boys let him go then, confident that he would tell the moment he got home but hoping he wouldn't. Violating all precedents, instead of going to the house as they always did, to see grandma and get nice things to eat, they turned right off down the road and went home even leaving the salt for the cattle in the pasture where any old cow could lick up all of it at once.*

When they got home their mother asked them how grandma was.

"She's well," lied Ernest

"Well, what was she doing. Tell me about her."

"O, just doin' same as always," said Eugene.

"Well, tell me about it," insisted their mother, but she could not get nothing more out of them.

After an hour or so, one of the lynchers "happened" to look up the road, which he had been watching all the time, and saw a negro man who lived on grandma's farm, swinging along at a good pace. He knew what they meant. Their crime had been discovered. Their mother was soon in nervous haste to go to grandma's because something had happened. "Why didn't you tell me grandma was sick?"she demanded, hastily getting ready. To Ernest, she said:

"Hitch up the buggy and drive me to grandma's."

"I'm sick," said the future conductor. "Make Gene go."

"Gene's got a chill and is in bed," said his mother, "and you go right along and hurry and hitch up."

"My stomach hurts," said Ernest. "My nose is going to bleed. I have a stone bruise on my left ear. My head aches somewhat awful. I can't go." But he had to go and went. During the drive he said not a word but looked sadly at the blue birds along the road, wishing he might have wings like they had and fly away from the trouble-some world.

Arriving at grandma's he found the little nigger in bed, all swathed up with rags around his neck, and the air was heavy with the smell of liniment. On the table Ernest saw candied apples, peach preserves, strawberries, quince preserves, blueberry jelly and other things that grandma always had on hand and his soul went sick thinking of all this rations being wasted on the little nigger whom he had almost hanged.

He looked around in the yard with misery all through him till the truth was found in all its glory, and he was taken back home.

"But I want you to remember," he said, as he yelled, "Uar-hee," that being the next station, "that Gene was the one who suggested the lynching and that he got a chill when the time came for another visit to go to grandma's."

"Well, did you get a licking for this lynching bee?" asked the writer.

"O. I got so many lickings along these times—though. Gene got more than I did because he was the meanest—I don't remember whether I got beat or not.

"All out for Bar-ber! Change cars for Winston-Salem."

CHAPTER 7
On the Lighter Side of Wickedness

DIFFERENT BUT INTERESTING REPORTING

I feel compelled to complete *Wicked Lexington, North Carolina* with a lighter tone and voice and mood. Some of the newspaper articles I have researched, though filled with less-than-happy events, are recorded in a rather humorous manner and bring a smile to my face. It's amazing how a misplaced modifier or ambiguous pronoun can change the meaning of a sentence. I want to share those with you, my readers, some of these happenings:

> Dispatch, August 13, 1936*: David Poston, young white man, is convicted of non-support and abandonment of his young wife and unborn child. He was sentenced to serve twelve months on the roads, suspended on condition he pay into the clerk's office the sum of $7 weekly for the use of his wife.*

> Dispatch, July 31, 1941: *George Floyd, white man, was found guilty of assault on a female, his sister-in-law Sallie Floyd, and given six months on the roads, suspended he not assault Sallie again for two years and pay the cost. The prosecution testified that she , the defendant, got into an argument and that he struck her with his fist. Floyd admitted striking the woman, but stated he did not use his fist, but just slapped her.*

> Article entitled "Little Sambo Hayes Breaks Collarbone," the Dispatch, July 31, 1941: *Several days after arriving at the beach more than two weeks ago, little Sambo Hayes, who is two and one-half years*

old was bouncing on the bed, lost his balance and fell against the screened window. The screen gave way and he fell out the window to the ground, breaking his left collar bone. He was taken to a baby specialist who has off hours in a hospital on the beach, and given treatment, and is getting along nicely, although he is still wearing adhesives.

"Kidnapping Case Fails But Poston Is Banished," the Dispatch, May 7, 1946: *"Dan and I had already planned to leave," nonchalantly testified Mrs. Jessie Wilson Hill, whose husband of a few hours had charged that Dan Poston kidnapped his bride late last Monday, when Poston was tried in County Court, Friday night on a series of charges growing out of the unusual incident.*

Dispatch, December 17, 1945: *Birdie Link was fined $10 and costs on an assault charge and prayer for judgment was continued for two years on condition she not again assault Mary Link.*

"False Alarm Boys Caught—Year Later," the Dispatch, January 4, 1958: *A year ago tomorrow night, firemen were called out here at 10 p.m. when a box alarm was turned in at the corner of Mendota Avenue and Farmer Street. There was no fire, and nobody could be found who knew anything about turning in the alarm. Yesterday police picked up two boys, 15 and 15, for questioning about other matters, and during the interrogation the boys admitted that they had turned in the false alarm a year earlier. They said they had been to the picture show, and were on their way home when one of them dared the other to turn in the alarm. This brought a return dare, and finally they compromised by turning in the alarm together.*

The boys also admitted using a .22 pistol to shoot holes in a tub owned by Jack Conner of South Lexington. Conner found out about the damage when he filled the tub with water. Police turned the boys over to the County Welfare Department, which will make disposition of the cases.

GHOSTS AND TRAMPS

Page S. Haynes wrote this amusing piece entitled "An Era of Only Ghosts and Tramps." It was published in the *Dispatch*, date unknown.

Most of the little kids were hauled by their parents to safe and sound Halloween carnivals, c. 1950, at local grammar schools, the annual trick or treat hold-up not having filtered down to the younger set.

I spent many early Oct. 31 nights at Robbins School, where to my awe, our classrooms were transformed into houses of horror, our teachers into assorted spooks and we were allowed to run down the hall.

Beloved Mrs. Owens of first grade fame appeared as an exotic Arabian fortune teller. "Your luckee color iss blue," she whispered with a hoarse accent. "Your luckee number, she iss seben and soon you weel meet a tall, dark and handsome stranger."

Miss Thompson's second-grade classroom was the highlight of the Robbins carnival, for it was converted into a true chamber of horrors. Eeries ghosts and witches (alias Miss Burgess and Miss Ledbetter, Mrs. Albright and Mrs. Curry) would lure us into its darkened interior, where we would be forced to feel corpse's eyeballs (grapes in Karo syrup) and guts (cold spaghetti). We'd crawl through the tunnel of terror, brushing up against sewer rats and snakes, being screeched at by bats and owls and finally, being scared witless at the exit where a howling dangly skeleton would block our way.

Funny, but the most horrifying episode of these ghost night entertainments was when little Jay Williams got his tongue frozen to a Fudgsicle, and all the grownups went running around panicky trying to get him unstuck without losing a layer of taste buds.

At age about 10 we pronounced ourselves too old for baby stuff...There was an honest-to-goodness haunted house across the street from me. We crept around to the back door, sneaked up on the porch and broke in to the kitchen. To this day I swear the table was set for two, with petrified servings of chicken, rice and peas, pots and pans were on the store and there was a rat family nested in the kitchen sink.

A brave couple of us ventured into the living room, where spider webs festooned the ceilings and windows and the furniture stood ghost-like, draped in white dust covers. A loud bang sent us all helter-skelter out the back door, across the street to the safety of my front hall. Panting and wide-eyed, we all agreed, "Shoot! That wasn't nothing but a car back-firing."

Courage regained, we ventured around the corner to the witch's house on Park Street. We knew she was a witch because she kept 15 cats and was always out on her front walk, sweeping with a broom. We sidled up to her front porch, where one intrepid member of the group (not me) put a brave foot on the step.

"Meeoowww, hisst, spiit," screeched 15 cats, as our witch came running out the door with her broom upended. "Get out'a here afore I call the police!" she bansheed at us.

Our Halloween trail always ended in the cemetery, but not far in, my friends, and not for long., Having been thoroughly schooled in the All Hallow's Eve tradition of spirits rising from their resting places at midnight, one of us, usually Tilly, would sight a wispy trail of white from behind the tree up yonder, scream bloody murder and it was take-off time again, heart a'pumping.

Later, under the covers (way under), I'd toss and turn, wondering what was going on up at the graveyard now, and what became of the unlucky couple across the street, who left their dinner uneaten, on the table.

1926 CONSPIRACY

The *Dispatch* reported this lawsuit: "John A. Pinch brings suits against brothers in Federal Court asking $300,000 damages charging them with conspiracy to incarcerate him in an insane asylum and seize his estate."

SLEAZY HORSE TRADER AND TRASHY SIDEWALKS

The October 1, 1913 issue of the *Dispatch* had these interesting and rather unusual reporting in the Local Items section:

Mr. E.B. Craven took a fall out of a horse trader yesterday when he got judgment against him for $200. He alleged and proved that one J.A. Dalton swapped him a worthless horse for his own good one, fraudulently concealing the defects of his horse and guaranteeing him sound in every particular. The defects complained of were not such as could be detected by the use of ordinary caution on the part of the buyer. The judgment was one that will enable the law to lay bold upon the person of Dalton, as well as upon his property, and full satisfaction for Mr. Craven is looked for.

At their last meeting the City Dads passed an ordinance requiring all merchants and business men to sweep the sidewalks in front of their places at least twice a week, one sweeping to take place Saturday night after the

> *business rush is over. If the slightest attention has been paid to this ordinance The* Dispatch *man has not see it. Sunday morning the sidewalks all over town were littered with trash. To our perennial, eternal question, "Where is a policemen?" let us add another: "Why is an ordinance?"*

Jug Breaking Concert: Swigging or Wholesome Fun?

> *The jug breaking and concert of the ladies of the Methodist church will take place in the opera house Friday night, August 7th. All parties holding jugs are requested to have them ready by next Thursday, as they will be called for on that day by the committee. Ice cream will be served during the breaking of the jugs at the opera house. An admission fee of 10 cents will be charged and everybody is cordially invited.*

Author's note: My research on jug breaking concerts turned up the following interesting information concerning the specifics of an 1877 event:

> *A jug is also called a flagon or handled jar with a spout, used for holding wine or other liquors.. But, there's more!*
>
> *Jug Breaking was a popular pastime at the turn of the eighteenth century, described as "a novel and creditable affair."*
>
> *After breaking the jugs with a hammer, one by one, dialogues, recitations, and singing were engaged in, when the sum in each jug was announced… All who had jugs, and children, were admitted free, but nevertheless the ten cent admissions amounted to $26.60, whilst this sum, added to the contents of the jogs, made the total proceeds of the enterprise $182.70, in 4764 pieces, from a five dollar bill downwards, weighing 41 pounds. The highest amount in any one jug was $14.42, and lowest, twenty-two cents. An interesting aside is the fact the Booker T. Washington mentions jug breaking to raise money for a school in 1883.*

So, this is definitely not a temperance story!

TO OUR CREDITORS

We have repeatedly sent you statements of your indebtedness to us and requested you to call and settle, but they have proved of no avail and we take this method of giving you this last notice that it you do not call and settle your account in full on or before September 1, 1901, we shall place same in the hands of our Attorney for immediate collection. Positively no exceptions made to this, as all Accounts will be treated alike. Please take notice and govern yourself accordingly. Respectfully, CLEMENT & HARGRAVE.

NOTHING NEW UNDER THE SUN

The August 5, 1903 issue of the *Dispatch* carried a short article entitled, "Some of Life's Perils." This piece probably could have been written today and been appropriate:

Drink water and get typhoid. Drink milk and get tuberculosis. Drink whiskey and get the jimjams. Drink soup and get Bright's disease. Eat meat and encourage apoplexy. Eat oysters and acquire toxemia. Eat vegetables and weaken the system. Eat dessert and take to paresis. Smoke cigarette and die early. Smoke cigars and get catarrh. Drink coffee and obtain nervous prostration. Drink wine and get the gout. In order to be entirely healthy one must eat nothing, drink nothing, smoke nothing, and even before breathing one should see that the air is properly sterilized.

SOME PROPOSED LAWS

The December 18, 1901 edition of the *Dispatch* printed the following platform set forth by P.J. Rucker, who announced his candidacy for the legislature:

"If I run for the house the fellow that beats me will have to get up and get, for the following laws I am going to pass: The farmer that plants corn closer than four or five feet apart put him in the penitentiary. Anyone that don't send their children to school as long as free school runs put them at the whipping post. Anyone that is not vaccinated put him in jail and vaccinate with pure smallpox. Any farmer that does not salt his hogs put him on the

chain gang for not salting his hogs because they are liable to cholera without salt. All farmers must raise corn and wheat enough to do them. If they don't I will put him to work in a blacksmith shop. If any man does not help his wife about the house on a rainy day or on Saturday he shall not have any dinner. If any lady cooks a man's victuals, when she announces that the meal is ready, any one of the family who does not come at once shall have his mouth filled with cold mush and a handkerchief tied over it to keep him from swallowing it. If any person complains of hard times put him in the penitentiary, the poor house and chain gang all at one time. No one has a right to complain of hard times. All bachelors over 40 years of age shall be hung. All old maids over thirty who have had five good chances to marry and refused them shall be sent to China as missionaries as a punishment for not marrying. The man that out talks his wife in a quarrel shall be shot. Any man whose wife has been dead for five years and he has not married again shall be paid a premium for he has shown plainly to the world that he needs it by not having enough sense to marry again. Every person shall have plenty of poultry, a good garden, two dozen or more Japanese plum trees, a grape arbor, pecan trees, a good peach and apple orchard. If he fails to have these he shall be sent to Africa. Any man that digs a well in his lot instead of doffing it near the house shall be made to draw all the water his wife needs, for he can run a trough from the well to the lot to water his stock. Any one that keeps his hog pens any closer than 200 yards of his dwelling house shall be made to sleep with them until he dies of typhoid fever. Any one that drinks whisky and don't put 90 per cent of water in it shall have his stomach lined with copper before he drinks it."

He Had to Go Home

This article appeared in the *Dispatch* on May 18, 1910:

A young man was spending the evening with his "best girl." About 10 o'clock a most terrific thunderstorm came up. The lightning flashed, the thunder rolled, and the rain came down in torrents. His prospective father-in-law entered the room on his way to the upper portion of the house, and said: "Charles, you must not think of going home in this storm. You would be wet through before you could hardly get started."

"But," protested Charles, "I do not like to put you to so much trouble."

"No trouble at all, Charles," put in the young lady. "I'll go at once and prepare a room for you. Excuse me for a short time, please." She was gone longer than she expected to and as she descended the front stairs was surprised to hear the outside door slam and to see Charles standing near it, dripping from head to feet. His hat was gone, and tightly clasped in his hand he held a small suit case.

"Why, Charles," she exclaimed in astonishment, "what did you go out for when it is raining so hard?"

"Well you see," replied Charles, "I just had to go home and get my nightshirt."

Hunter Leaves Obscene Note

Apparently a trespassing hunter did not like being asked to leave. The *Dispatch* reported this rather unusual event in the October 22, 1948 issue. The caption read, "Will Swear Out Warrant. Writes Note to Hunter Gets Obscene Answer," and this is what transpired:

F.A. Wilson, well known dairyman of near Welcome, was in town this morning for the purpose of swearing out a warrant for a hunter who he alleges trespassed on his property and then left an obscene note hanging on a haystack pole at his farm.

Mr. Wilson stated that he would swear out the warrant for an Erlanger man who he alleges trespassed on his farm Tuesday, October 19, for the purpose of hunting squirrels. Mr. Wilson declared that another man was along at the time and that as soon as he could secure his name that he would swear out another warrant. Mr. Wilson said that he secured the license number of the car.

Wilson had the note with him this morning. He himself had left a note on the windshield of the hunters' car reading, "do you want to look me up or do you want the law to look you up?" Yesterday while touring his farm with Fred Wilson of this city, Mr. Wilson found the vulgar reply.

Mr. Wilson stated that he had watched the two young men hunting in the woods near a field on his farm. He said that he blocked the road leading out of the field and had a talk with one of the young men last Tuesday.

"We farmers do not like for persons to trespass on our farms for hunting purposes. I do not like many people hunting on my farm and those that do must have permission," he declared. "In the future I plan to take our warrants for anyone else hunting on my land without permission," he emphasized heatedly.

Hundred-Dollar Penalty for Writing Too Much

In the *Dispatch*'s December 20, 1911 edition, this detailed article, entitled "New Ruling Made in Postoffice [*sic*] Department," clarifies its change in policy:

> *Stamps other than the regular United States postage stamps must not appear on the face of packages: that the back of the package is the proper place for such stamps. This is a ruling that went into effect since last Christmas.*
>
> *Packages cannot be accepted which bear stamps which seal any of the folds of the package so that they cannot be opened for inspection, if necessary, without breaking the seal or stamp.*
>
> *The officials recommend more care in the wrapping of packages as many weak strings and inferior paper, sometimes with a bow-knot when as a matter of safety it should be a hard knot.*
>
> *A new ruling of the postoffice department makes permissible the following words on the outside of the package: "Please do not open until Christmas." Last year such an inscription made the package subject to first-class postage. The name of the sender of a package is allowed therein together with the words, "Christmas greetings." When small packages are enclosed in a larger one the name of the persons for whom each smaller package is intended is permissible.*
>
> *The person writing more than this in a package is subject to a penalty of $100 which has been raised within the last year from $10.*

Excessive Timidity

This short article, entitled "To Overcome Bashfulness," was presented as a true Lexington tale in the January 31, 1906 local newspaper:

> *An ordinarily truthful man deposes and such that the following is true to the best of his knowledge and belief.*
>
> *A bashful Davidson county lover, very bashful, one night last summer attended an ice cream party in the country and had the splendid chance of "seeing" a pretty girl to her home. He allowed the opportunity to go unimproved, however, because of his excessive timidity. It rankled in his mind that night—made him made to think that he was so backward. The next morning he was in the field plowing, when a passer-by saw him take*

the line from the house and tie himself with it to a tree. Then he began whipping himself soundly, cussing the while. "D——ye! Why didn't ye buck up to that girl last night. D——ye, air ye goin to buck up to the next pretty girl ye git a chance to, huh?" And the eavesdropper went on his way to spread the news.

APPENDIX

Old Lexington Recipes

These are all recipes given to me by Lexington family and friends. I cannot give individual credit because I have been preparing these dishes, breads and desserts for many years. Most of the recipes are written on now worn and tattered index cards. A few were typed on an old Underwood or Royal. Some were given to me by my paternal grandmother who ran a boardinghouse in Lexington. I have been cooking or baking since I was very young, standing on a stool in the kitchen. About my only claim to fame in the culinary circle would be the Betty Crocker Homemaker of America award that I won when I was a freshman at Lexington Senior High School. Enjoy.

Eunice Fritts's Barbecued Chicken

3 tbsp. catsup
3 tbsp. vinegar
2 tbsp. water
3 tbsp. brown sugar
3 tbsp. prepared mustard
1 tsp. salt
1 tbsp. real butter, melted
3 tbsp. Worcestershire sauce
Juice of ½ lemon
1 tsp. red pepper (or Texas Pete)
3–4 lb. chicken, cut in serving pieces

Combine first 10 ingredients. Cook sauce on top of stove until everything is blended well. Let cool. Dip each piece of chicken into sauce. Place in baking dish lined with aluminum foil and pour the remainder of sauce over chicken. Cook in oven 3 hours at 300 degrees.

AUNT MARY NOBLE'S WALDORF ASTORIA CHOCOLATE CAKE

½ cup butter
2 cups sugar
4 squares chocolate, melted
2 eggs
2 cups sifted cake flour
2 tsp. baking powder
1½ cups milk
2 tsp. vanilla
1 cup nuts, optional

Cream butter and sugar. Add melted chocolate and well-beaten eggs. Sift dry ingredients together and add alternately with milk. Add vanilla and nuts. Bake in chosen pan(s) at 350 degrees for about 1 hour. (Batter will be very thin, but this is the way it is supposed to be.)

Icing for cake:
½ cup butter
2 squares chocolate, melted
1 egg, well beaten
1½ cups powdered sugar
1 tsp. vanilla
1 tsp. lemon juice
½ cup nuts (optional)

Melt butter and add chocolate; add egg; stir in sugar. Add vanilla, lemon juice, and nuts and beat until smooth.

MY MOTHER'S FRIEND'S CHICKEN AND PASTA CASSEROLE

1 chicken fryer, cut up
Flour
1 can cream of celery soup
Canned chicken broth, optional

½ lb. angel hair spaghetti
½ cup chopped green or red pepper
8 oz. canned mushroom pieces
Salt and pepper to taste.
2 cups shredded cheddar cheese (I use more)
1 small 3 oz. jar pimento

Cook chicken until tender. Save broth. Take chicken off the bone and break into small pieces. Thicken broth with flour. Add soup and blend well. You should have 4 cups. If not, add some canned chicken broth.
Cook spaghetti until almost done—should still be a little hard. Now layer in 9- by 13-inch baking dish, sprayed with Pam, as follows: ½ spaghetti, ½ the chopped pepper, ½ the chicken, ½ the mushrooms, and ½ the soup mixture and pimento. Sprinkle with salt and pepper and top with ½ of the cheese. Repeat layers; cover with foil and bake 350 degrees for 20–30 minutes or until heated throughout and cheese is melted.

LES'S MOTHER'S FRUITCAKE

2 sticks margarine
1 box light brown sugar
2 cups granulated sugar
9 eggs
1 small can crushed pineapple
4 cups self-rising flour
1 orange
3 apples
4 bananas
1 box white raisins
1 small box dates
2 lbs. mixed fruit (I use only cherries and pineapple)
4 cups pecans
1 tsp. cinnamon
1 tsp. nutmeg
1 small coconut (ground or grated)
2 tsp. vanilla extract

Cream margarine and sugar. Add well-beaten eggs. Add crushed pineapple. Then add flour (save enough flour to dredge fruit). Mix well and add all other fruits, nuts, spices, coconut and vanilla. Bake in tube pans at 300 degrees until done—approximately 3 hours. This makes two wicked cakes!

AUNT REENIE GAMBRELL'S SQUASH CASSEROLE

1 stick real butter
1 pkg. Pepperidge Farm Herb dressing
1½ to 2 lbs. fresh summer squash
1 large carrot, grated
½ onion, grated
Small amount pimento (½ of 15-cent bottle)
½ pint sour cream
1 can cream chicken soup

Melt butter, add Pepperidge Farm dressing and mix well. Stew squash until tender. Add grated carrot, onion, pimento, sour cream and chicken soup. Mix thoroughly, but do not beat. Put ½ of dressing in bottom of baking dish and then add squash mixture. Put other half of dressing mix on top. Bake 350 degrees for 35–40 minutes until golden brown.

MRS. ARNOLD BECK'S WATERGATE SALAD

1 pkg. pistachio instant pudding (3.4 oz) mix
1 can (20 oz.) crushed pineapple, with juice
1½ cups miniature marshmallows
8 ounces Cool Whip

Mix together and chill in refrigerator.

GRANDMOTHER EVANS'S BOILED CUSTARD

4 eggs
1 cup sugar
1 quart milk
1 tsp. vanilla

Beat eggs with sugar. Heat milk in double boiler. When hot, add a little milk to the eggs and sugar. Then add all to the milk in the double boiler. Cook until thickened slightly. Remove from heat and stir in vanilla. Refrigerate. It will thicken more as it cools.
Grandmother's hint: Test by sticking spoon in mixture. If it coats spoon, stop cooking. Stir constantly (maybe 30 minutes).

Aunt Mabel Koonts's Russian Tea

1 tbsp. allspice
1 tbsp. cloves
2 cups sugar
8 cups cold water
8 fresh oranges
1 lemon
Large can of pineapple juice

Mix allspice, cloves, sugar and water. Add juice of oranges and lemon. Then add pineapple juice. Keep in big jar in refrigerator. Heat amount needed for serving.

Lemon Sheet Cake

1 package (18¼ oz.) lemon cake mix
4 eggs
1 can (15¾ oz.) lemon pie filling
1 package (3 oz.) cream cheese, softened
½ cup butter or margarine, softened
2 cups confectioner's sugar
1½ tsp. vanilla extract

In a large mixing bowl, beat the cake mix and eggs until well blended. Fold in pie filling. Spread into a greased 15- by 10-inch baking pan. Bake at 350 degrees for 18–20 minutes or until a toothpick inserted near the center comes out clean. Cool on a wire rack.

In a small mixing bowl, beat cream cheese, butter and confectioner's sugar until smooth. Stir in vanilla. Spread over cake. Store in refrigerator.

Anita's Okra and Tomatoes

1 lb. tiny, tender fresh okra
¾ cup chopped onion
¼ cup chopped green peppers
2 cloves minced garlic
2 tbsp. vegetable oil
2 ripe country tomatoes, peeled and coarsely chopped
½ tsp. salt
½ tsp. pepper
¼ cup water
Dash of hot sauce

Wash okra and drain. Remove tips and stems. Cook onion, green pepper and garlic in a large skillet over medium heat, stirring constantly. Add okra and remaining ingredients. Bring to a boil. Cover, reduce heat and simmer 25 minutes, stirring occasionally.

Coconut Sour Cream Cake

1 (18½ oz.) package butter-flavored cake mix
2 cups sugar
1 (16 oz.) carton sour cream
1 (12 oz.) package frozen coconut, thawed
1½ cups frozen whipped topping, thawed

Prepare cake mix by package directions, making two 8-inch layers. When cool, split both layers (to make 4). Combine sugar, sour cream and coconut, blending well; chill. Reserve 1 cup sour cream mixture for frosting; spread remainder between layers of cake. Combine reserved sour cream mixture with whipped topping. Blend until smooth. Spread on top and sides of cake. Seal cake in airtight container and refrigerate for 3 days before serving.

Sister Ann's Cheesy Appetizer

1 large onion, chopped
1 clove garlic, minced
1 tbsp. vegetable oil
1 tbsp. flour
1 tbsp. chili powder
1 10 oz. can tomatoes and green chiles
1 chopped jalapeno pepper
1 lb. Velveeta cheese

Sauté onion and garlic in oil until transparent. Add flour and chili powder. Cook 1 minute. Add can of tomatoes and green chiles and cook until sauce is thickened. Add jalapeno pepper. Add cheese in chunks and cook until melted. Serve hot in chafing dish with tortilla chips

Davis Townsend School Meatloaf

2 lbs. ground beef
2 cups bread crumbs (about 4 slices)
2 eggs

½ cup catsup
2 tbsp. mustard
½ tsp. salt
¼ tsp. pepper
⅔ cup canned milk
3 tbsp. real butter
Chopped onion (a lot or a little)

With clean hands, mix everything together and bake at 400 degrees for 1 hour or until brown on top.

LEMON CHESS PIE

2 cups sugar
1 tbsp. flour
2 tbsp. self-rising cornmeal
4 eggs, well-beaten
½ cup butter, melted
¼ cup milk
¼ cup lemon juice
4 tsp. grated lemon rind
2 9-inch pie crusts, baked for 10 minutes at 350 degrees

Mix sugar, flour and cornmeal; add to eggs, beating well. Add butter, milk, lemon juice and rind, mixing well. Pour into pie crusts and bake at 350 degrees for 45 minutes. Makes 2 pies. Eat one and freeze the other!

ELIXIR FOR JOINTS, ACHES AND PAINS ASSOCIATED WITH ARTHRITIS

1 12 oz. can unsweetened apple juice (frozen)
1 12 oz. can unsweetened grape juice (frozen)
1 cup apple cider vinegar
6–7 oz. honey
6 12 oz. juice cans of water

Mix well. Refrigerate. Drink 2–3 oz. (or more) daily.

CHICKEN SWISS

4 boneless chicken breasts
Garlic powder
Salt and pepper to taste
1 8 oz. package Swiss cheese
½ cup white wine
1 can cream of mushroom soup
½ package herb seasoned dressing mix
½ stick butter, melted.

Rub chicken with garlic powder, salt and pepper. Place in a buttered baking dish and cover with cheese. Mix wine and soup and pour over chicken. Sprinkle with dressing mix; then dribble with butter. Bake 325 degrees for 45 minutes.

Bibliography

Baity, Glen. "Local Fans Remember the Day Elvis Came to Town." *Dispatch*, March 21, 2006.

Capel, Wint. *The Good Doctor's Downfall.* Lincoln, NE: iUniverse, Inc., 2004.

Daniel, Jim. *The Early Court Houses of Davidson County, North Carolina.* Lexington, NC: Davidson County Historical Museum, Lexington, 2008.

Dispatch. Advertisements. August 13, 1936.

———. "Another Driver Is Charged With Embezzlement: Leroy Best Under Bond: Probation Probably in Cloth Theft At Mill." December 17, 1945.

———. "Anti-Shoplifting Clinic Set." November 7, 1960.

———. "Blood Analysis Is Being Made at Chapel Hill: Shirt Found Last Night Proves the Lead Sought." August 19, 1936.

———. "Carnival Men Assist in Arrest of Diner Thief Here This Morn." July 22, 1949.

———. "Charlie Chaplin." April 17, 1918.

———. "Children Under 16 Must Have Work Permits." August 19, 1936.

———. "Churchmen Urge Members To Refuse To See Dirty Films." December 2, 1960.

———. "Davidson Jury Acquits Farmer in Assault Case: Rejects Girl's Story of Attack Upon her by Brother-in-law." February 4, 1935.

———. "Elvis Presley Show—Performer Draws Huge Attendance." March 22, 1956.

———. "Enoch Truitt Is Accused Of Rape." August 16, 1948.

———. "He Had to Go Home." May 18, 1910.

———. "Jake Everhart Surrenders." September 2, 1903.
———. "Jug Breaking Concert." August 5, 1903.
———. "Local Items." April 17, 1918.
———. "Local Items." October 1, 1913.
———. "Man Charged with Forgery Arrested Here." August 13, 1936.
———. "Man Is Alleged Leader of Shoplifting Youths." February 7, 1956.
———. "Moonshine." February 28, 1947.
———. "Motive Revealed; Murder Gun Found." August 19, 1936.
———. "Negro Continues to Deny Murder." August 15, 1951.
———. "Negro Held in Hinshaw Murder." April 14, 1951.
———. "Negro Made Threats. Said He Would Kill White Boss and Then Fled and Was Taken After Hot Chase." October 10, 1905.
———. "Negro Murdered in Boone Township. Walter Simmons Shot Ernest Smith. A Negro 'Festibule' the Place and Corn Liquor the Cause." August 12, 1903.
———. "New Ruling Made in Postoffice Department." December 20, 1911.
———. "No Pool Rooms Will Be Licensed After August 1." April 17, 1918.
———. "Obscene Mail Menace Growing." May 20, 1959.
———. "Odell James Held to Higher Court in Assault Case." September 11, 1947.
———. "Prisoner Uses Razor and Gun In County Jail: Two Cut When Negress Goes Wild—Pistol Fails to Fire." May 8, 1930.
———. "Proceedings of the Court." September 2, 1903.
———. "Roman Charged." August 16, 1951.
———. "Sentence Suspended On Shoplifting Charge." February 16, 1959.
———. "Some Proposed Laws. Executed by a Possible Candidate for the Legislature." December 18, 1901.
———. "The Story of a Lynching." April 14, 1909.
———. "Taxicab Driver Arrested For Embezzlement." September 29, 1949.
———. "Thirteen Polio Cases Set Record For This County." June 22, 1948.
———. "To Our Creditors." July 17, 1901.
———. "To Overcome Bashfulness." January 31, 1906.
———. "Two Arrested as Wild Drive through City Is Blocked." September 5, 1932.
———. "Two More Cases Polio Reported Since Thursday." August 15, 1948.
———. "Was She Beaten to Death?" August 12, 1903.
———. "What Became of the Chief?" April 17, 1918.

———. "White Slave Traffic. An Ugly-Looking Case Close Home—Trial Postponed Until Monday Afternoon at Four." July 5, 1911.

———. "Will Swear Out Warrant. Writes Note to Hunter, Gets Obscene Answer." October 22, 1948.

———. "Woman Brutally Murdered." August 13, 1951.

———. "Younce and Brinkley Will Tell Truth." February 6, 1932

Geringer, Joseph: "Nannie Doss: Lonely Hearts Lady Loved Her Man to Death." truTV.com, http://www.trutv.com/library/crime/notorious_murders/women/doss/1.html (accessed January 29, 2011).

Haynes, Page S. "An Era of Only Ghosts and Tramps." *Dispatch*, n.d.

HistoryNet.com. "Annie Oakley." http://www.historynet.com/annie-oakley.htm (accessed January 29, 2011).

Lincoln University. "McRary Hall." http://02bee66.netsolhost.com/residencelife/index.php?option=com_content&view=article& (accessed February 9, 2011).

Moore, Scotty. "YMCA Gymnasium, Lexington, NC." ScottyMoore.net, http:www.scottymoore.net/lexington.html (accessed January 29, 2011).

Moose, Charles A., and Charles Fleming. *Three Weeks in October: The Manhunts for the Serial Sniper.* New York: Dutton, 2003.

New York Times. "Accuses Wife and Negro: North Carolina Editor Asks Divorce and $1000.00." http://query.nytimes.com/gst/abstract.html?res=9D03E4DC1F31E03ABC4F52DFBE66838 (accessed February 9, 2011).

Prince, James D. *The Day Elvis Came to Town.* Lexington, NC: Southern Heritage Publishing, 1995.

Sink, Joe. "A Tue Story About Men Killing Each Other." Speech, Lexington, North Carolina, O. Henry Study Club. Fall 2010.

"Turn Back the Clock: Brutal Murder Led Davidson County Man To Execution." Unpublished column.

Waymarking.com. "The Homestead, Unexpected Houseguests—Lexington NC—Civil War Discovery Trail Sites." http://www.waymarking.com/waymarks/WM5G1Y_The_Homestead_Unexpected_Houseg...%5b (accessed February 5, 2011).

Wikipedia. "Hugh Judson Kilpatrick." http://en.wikipedia.org/wiki/Hugh_Judson_Kilpatrick (accessed February 5, 2011).

———. "Nannie Doss." http://en.wikipedia.org/wiki/Nannie_Doss (accessed January 29, 2011).

York's Historical Connection. "Jug Breaking." and "York Methodists Break Jugs – Universal York." http://www.yorkblog.com/universal/2008/01/jug-breaking-for-fun-and-profi.html (accessed February 22, 2011).

Young, Franklin. "From Tizzy to Frantic, Teenagers Dig Performer at Lexington 'Y.'" *Salisbury Post*, March 22, 1956.

About the Author

Alice E. Sink is the published author of numerous nonfiction and fiction books, short stories, articles and essays. She earned her master's of fine arts in creative writing from the University of North Carolina Greensboro. For thirty years she taught writing courses at High Point University in High Point, North Carolina, where she received the Meredith Clark Slane Distinguished Teaching/ Service Award in 2002. The North Carolina Arts Council and the partnering arts councils of the Central Piedmont Regional Artists Hub Program awarded Sink a 2007 grant to promote her writing. She lives in Kernersville, North Carolina, with her husband, Tom, and their rescued dogs and cats.